NO!

ant's

RULE!

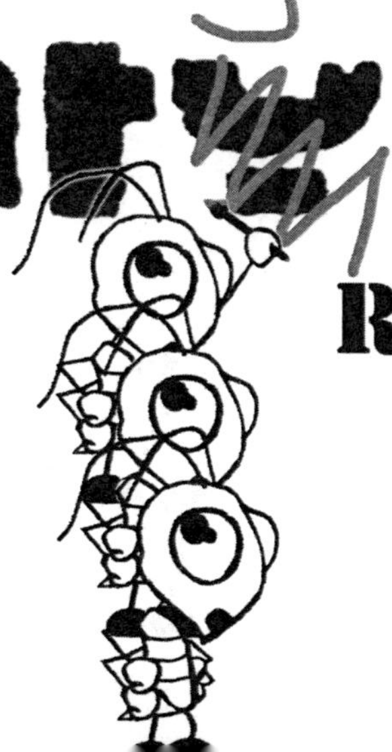

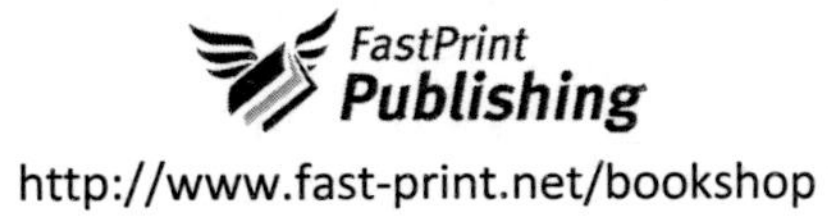

http://www.fast-print.net/bookshop

WHAT A MISTAKE: DESIGN & ARTWORK

A catalogue record for this book is available from the British Library

ISBN 978-178456-284-7

First published 2015 by
FASTPRINT PUBLISHING
Peterborough, England.

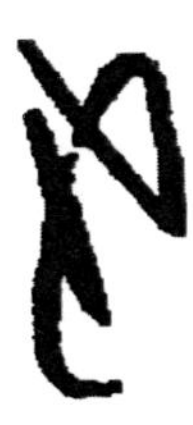

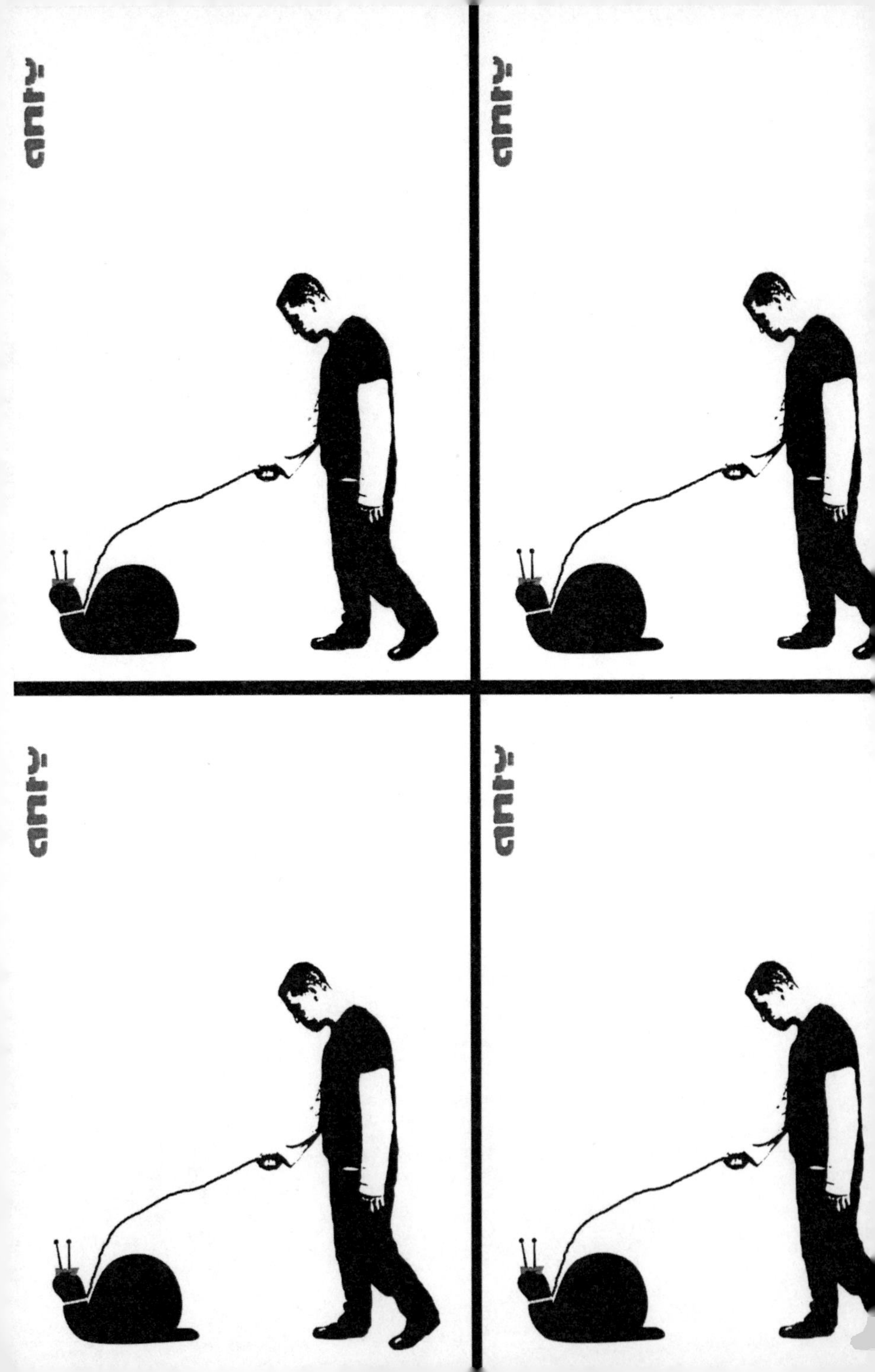

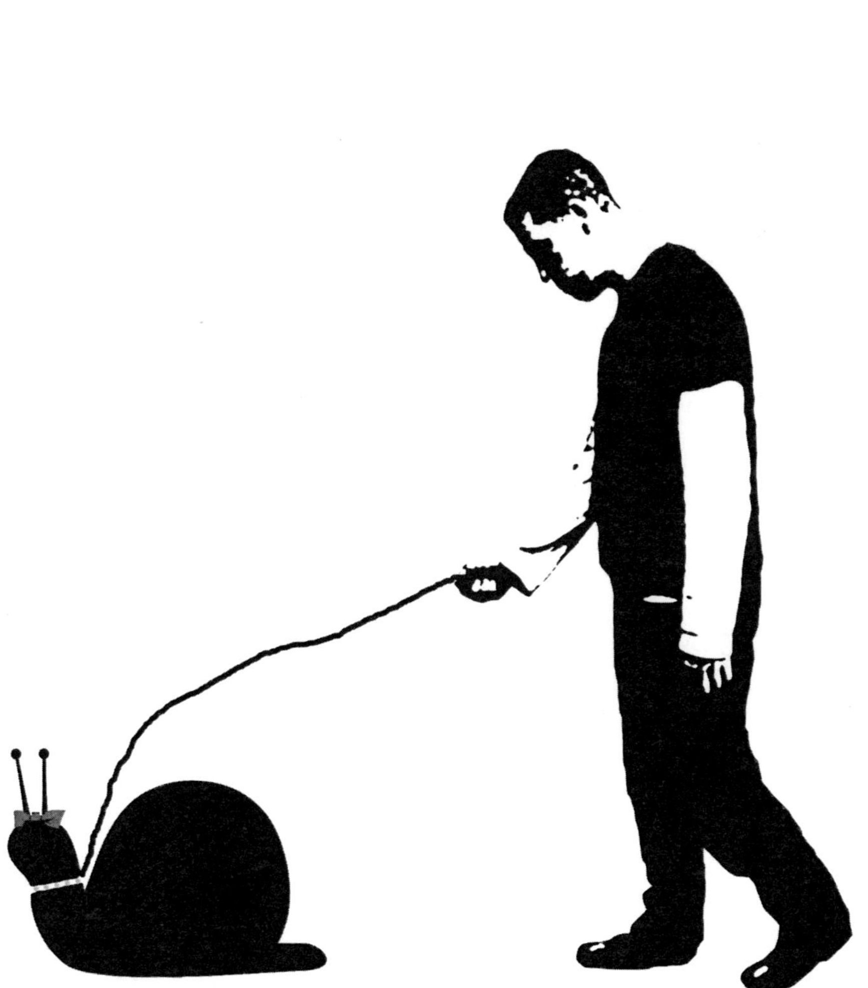

Don't

judge

me

I am So Random Its Unreal I Always get questioned about my work and what goes through my head!

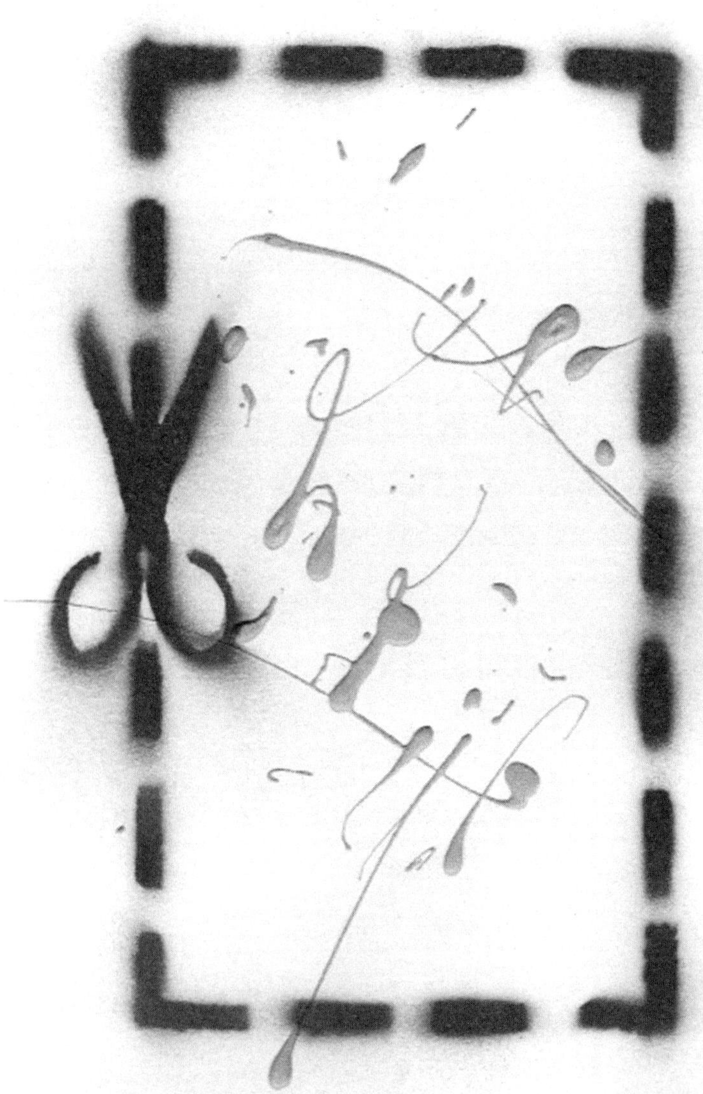

arty

I Like Cutting Crap Out Of Things
thats why the image on your left is
an Example of Cutting Crap!

Everyone Seems To Cut The Crap!

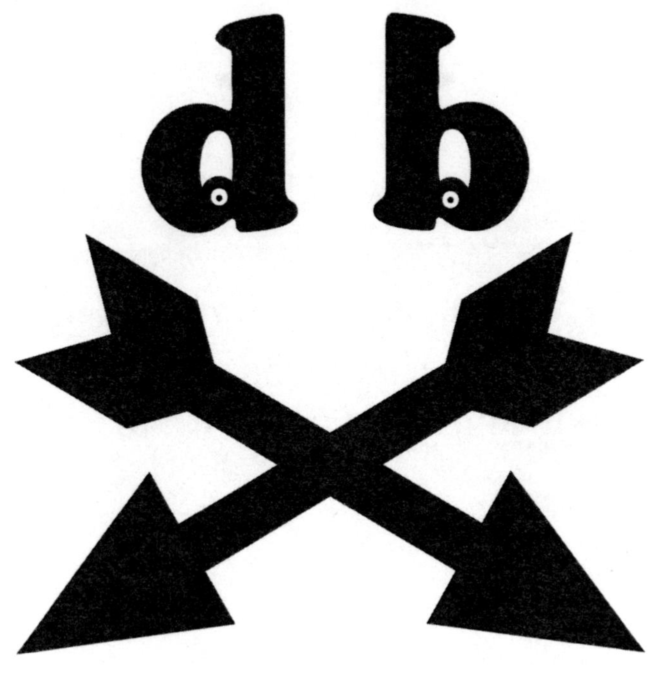

Ideas Always Pop In My Head I Really Don't Know The Meaning Of This one!

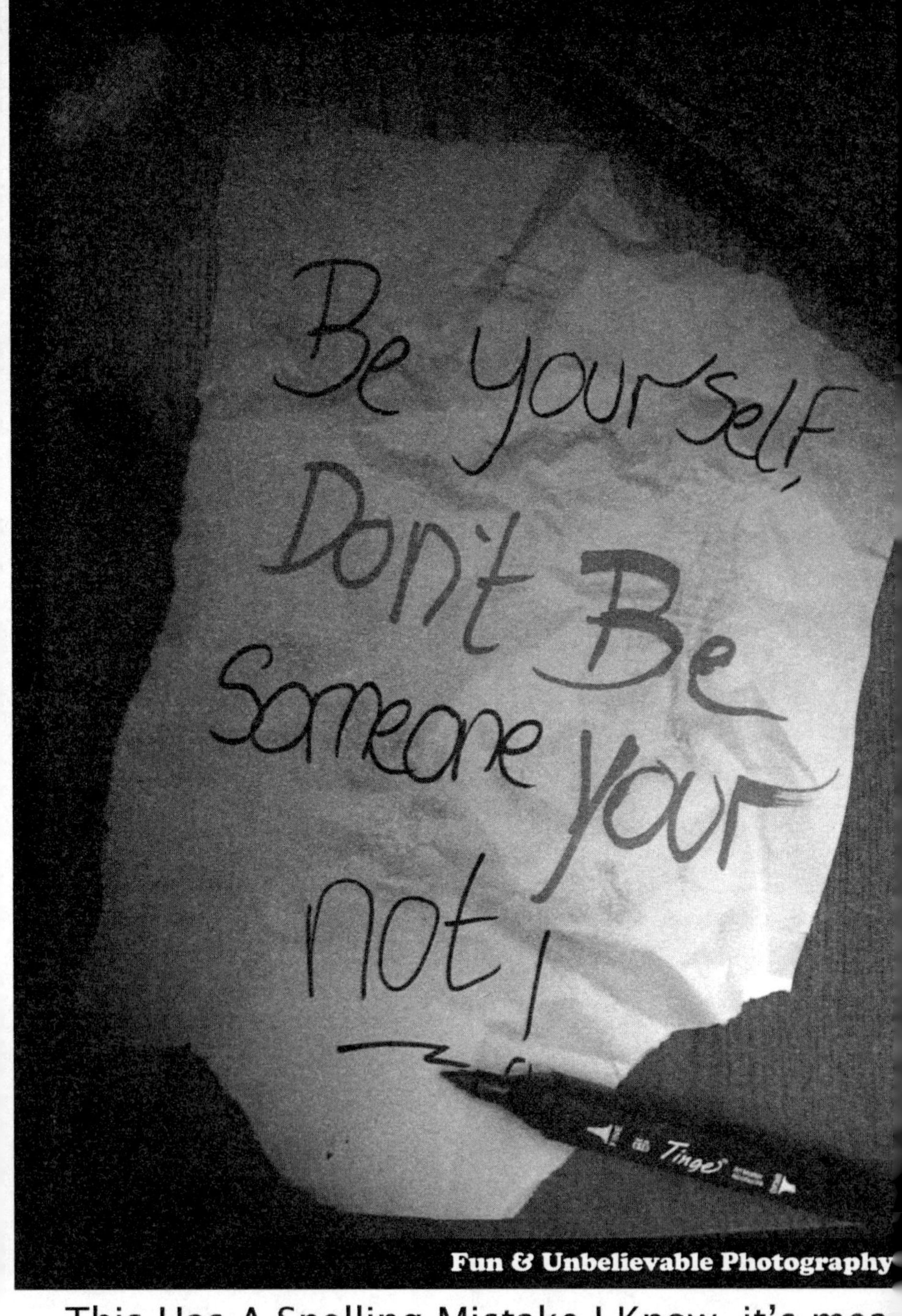

This Has A Spelling Mistake I Know, it's mea
to say You're Instead of Your!

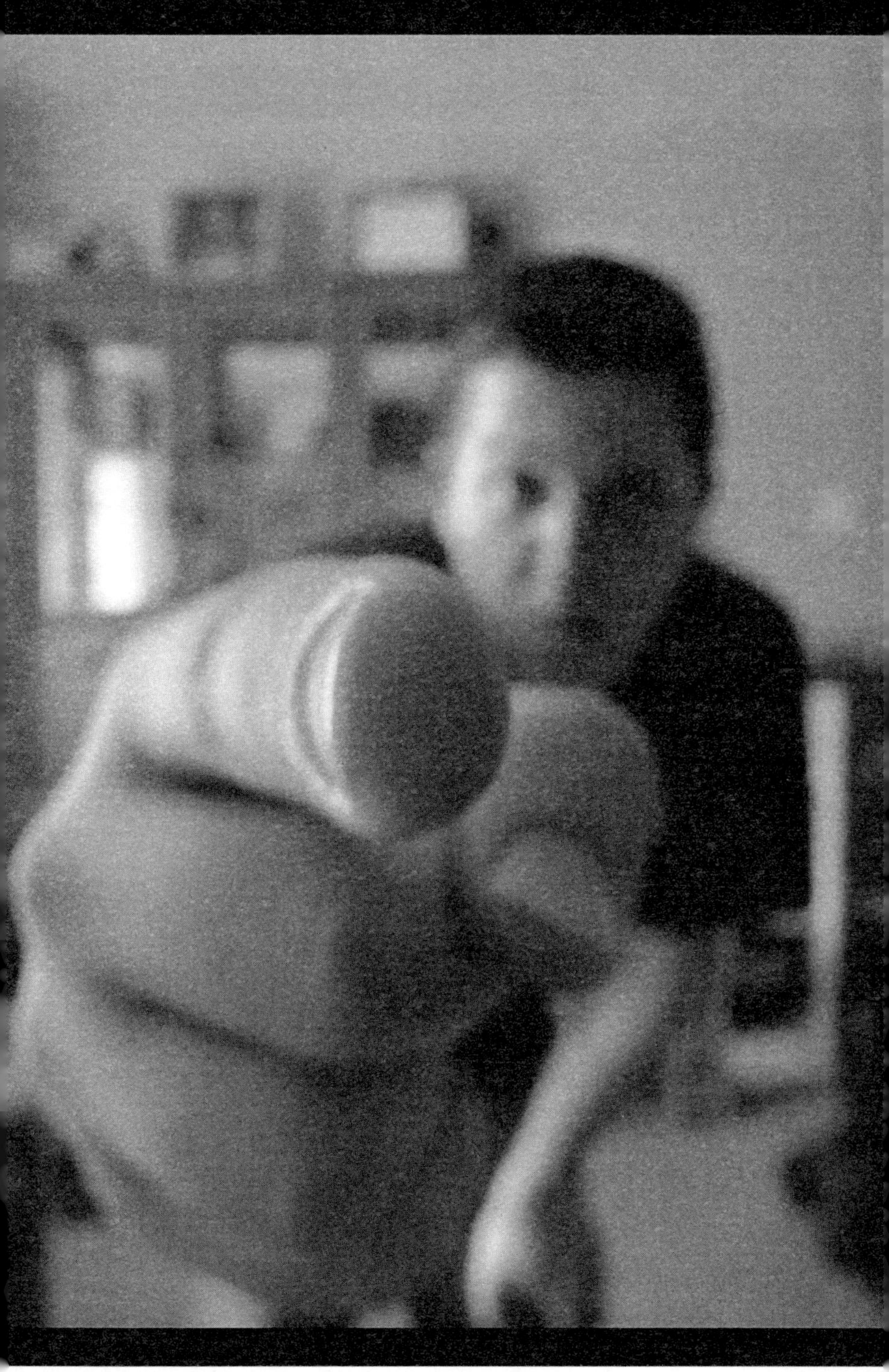

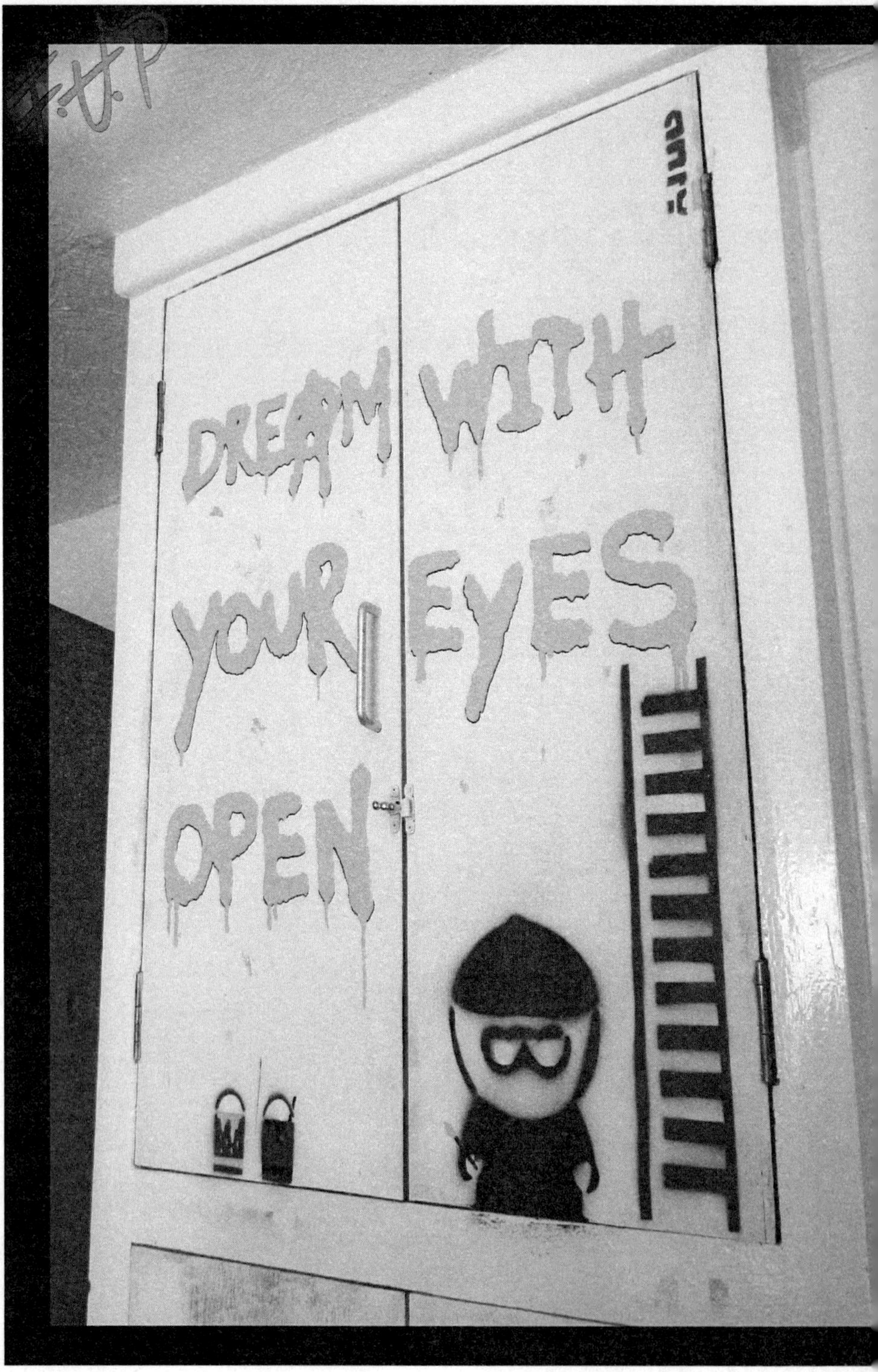

DREAM WITH
YOUR EYES
OPEN

YOU SHOULD ALWAYS LIVE YOUR DREAMS
ON'T CLOSE YOUR EYES DREAM WITH THEM
OPEN!

All you need to know about me as a persor

1) Creavtive!
2) Artistic!
3) Imagineative!
4) RANDOMNESS!!!!!!

Hope You Guys Are Enjoying The Book So Far If Your Not Then You Can Use It As Loo Roll, At Least Your Getting Your Money's Worth!

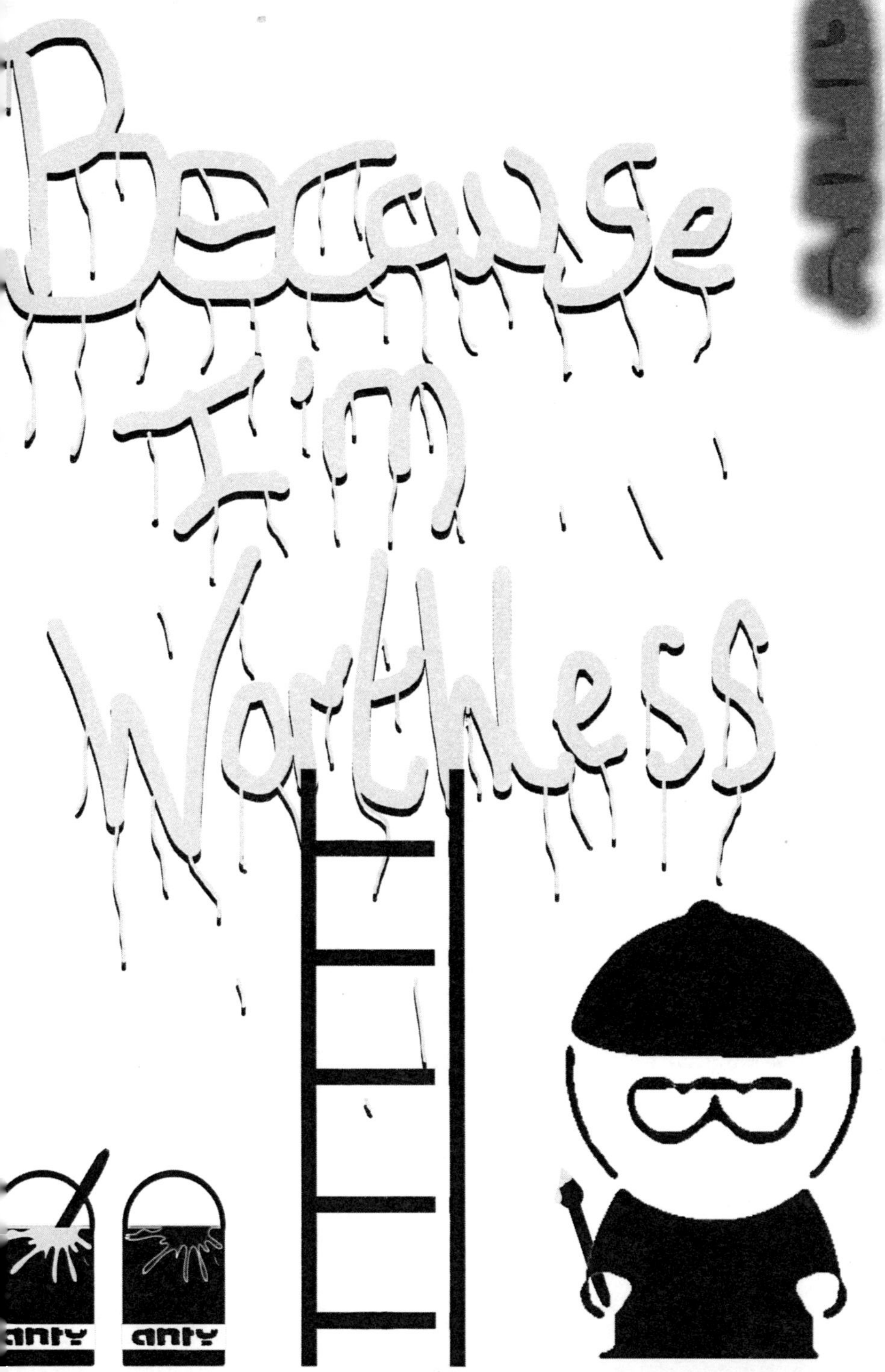
Because
I'm
Worthless
anty
anty

This T-Shirt Design Has No Meaning Its Just As Random As I Am!

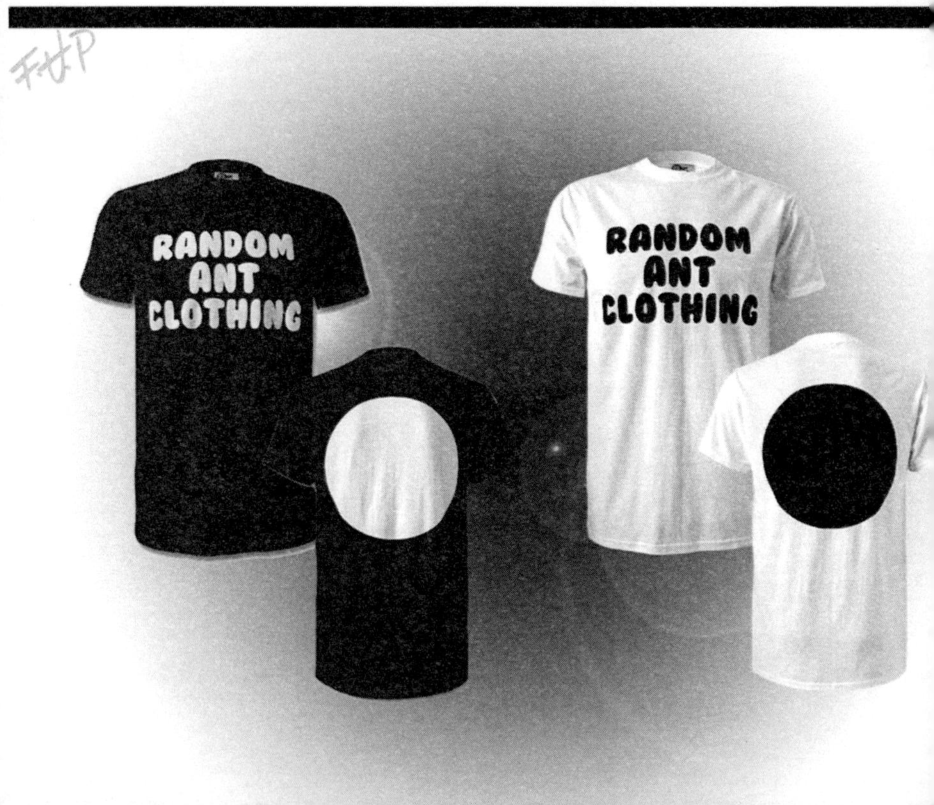

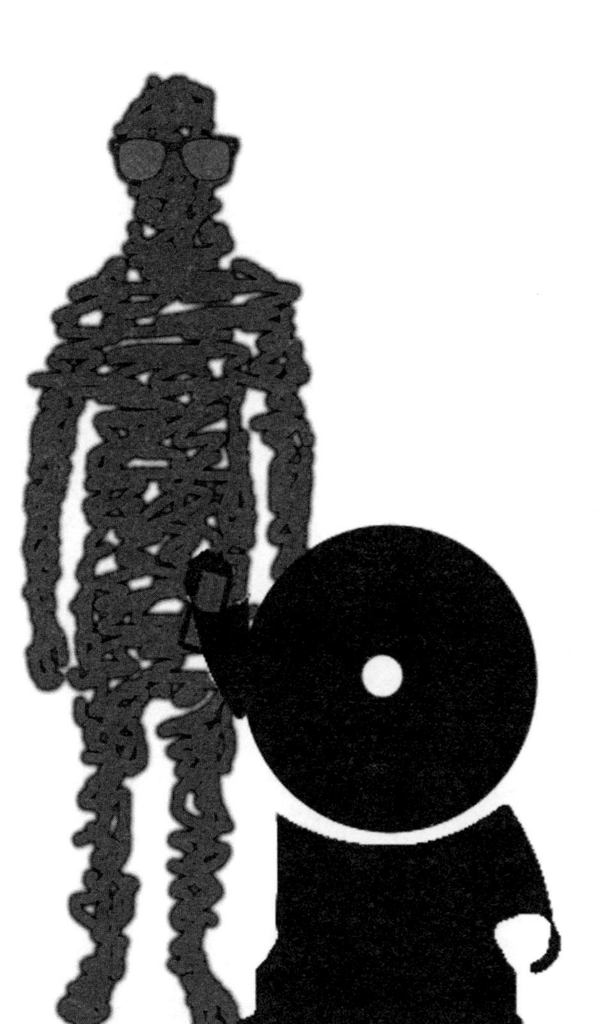

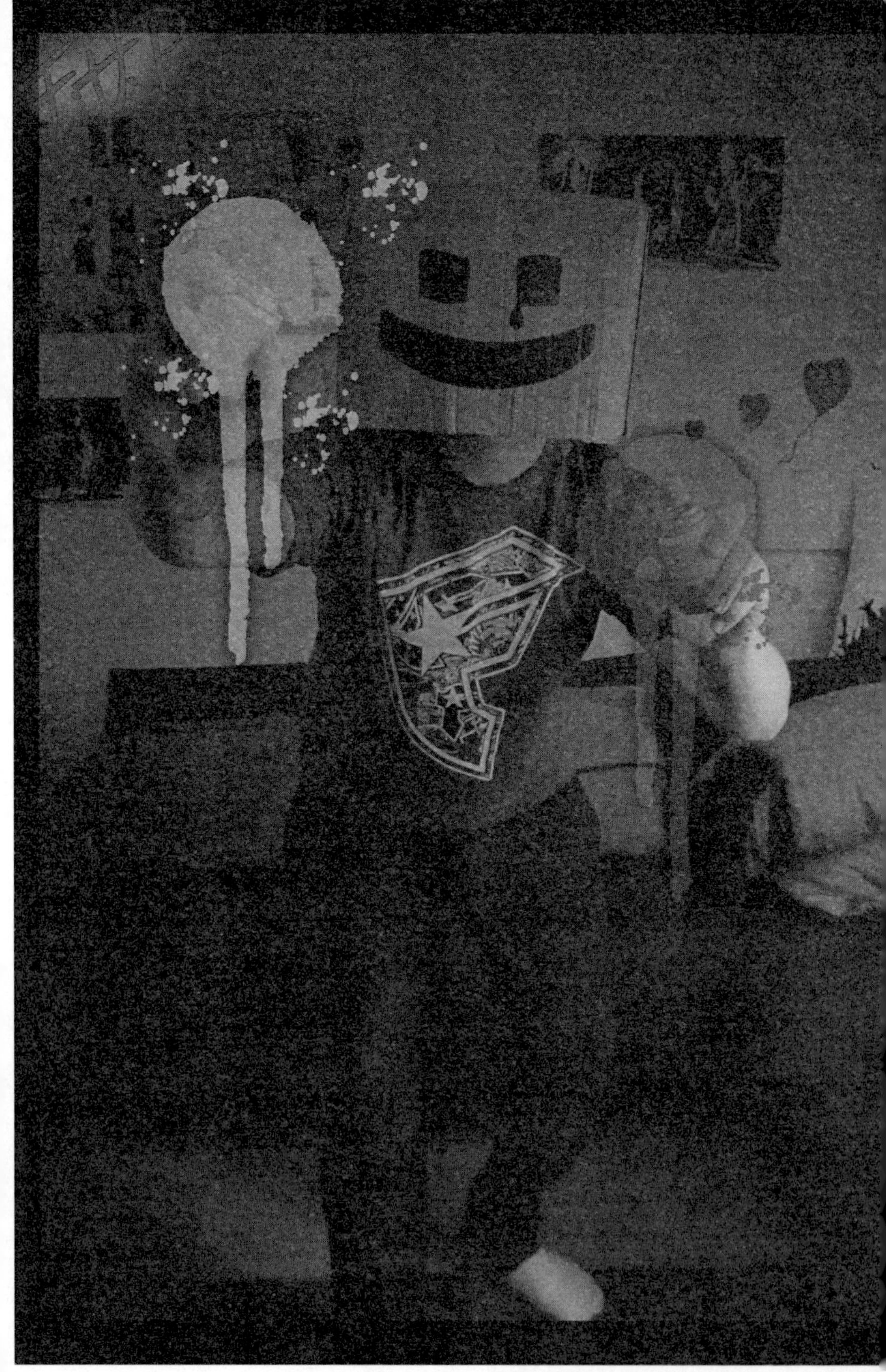

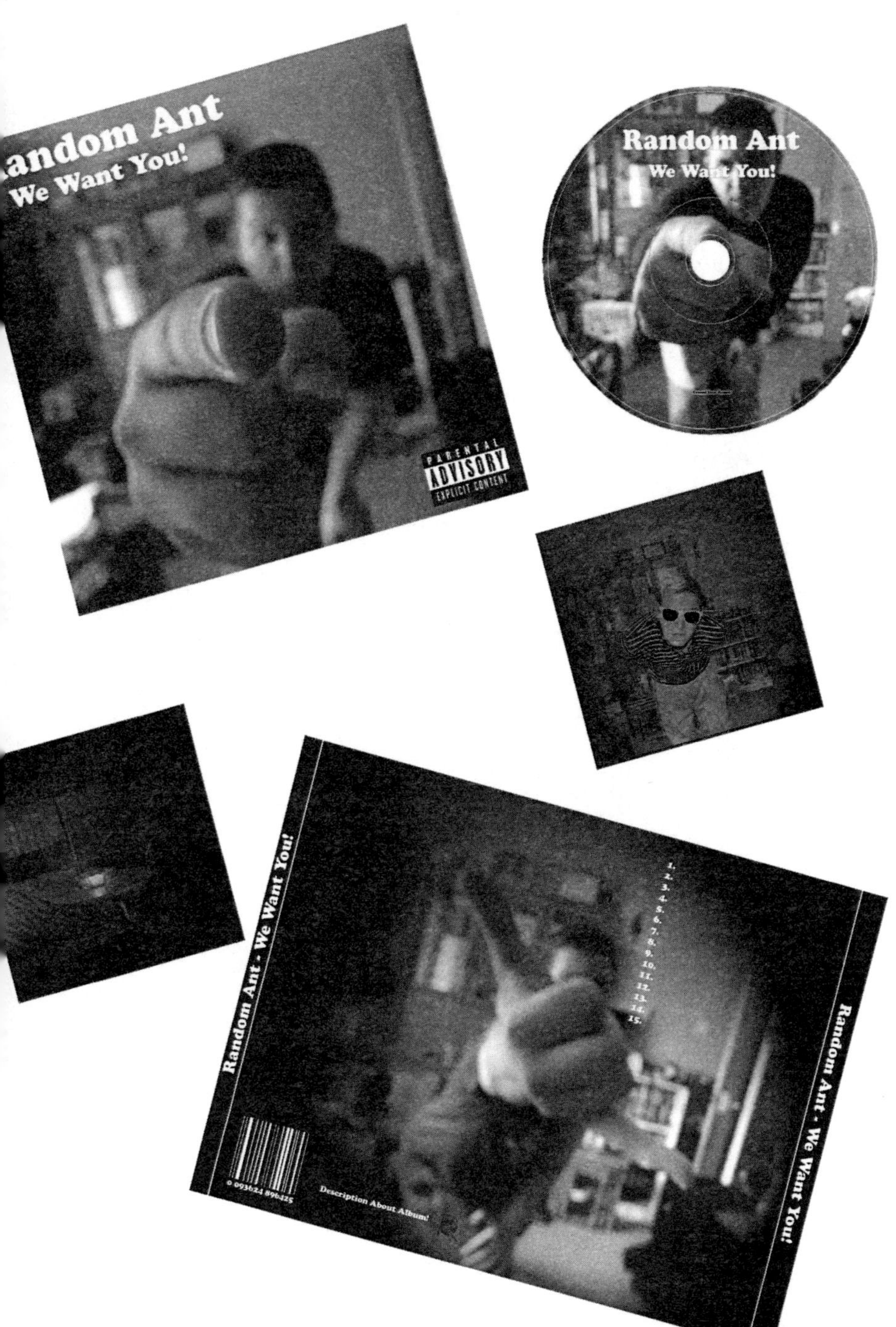
andom Ant
We Want You!
PARENTAL
ADVISORY
EXPLICIT CONTENT
Random Ant
We Want You!
Random Ant - We Want You!
1.
2.
3.
4.
5.
6.
7.
8.
9.
10.
11.
12.
13.
14.
15.
0 093624 896425
Description About Album!
Random Ant - We Want You!

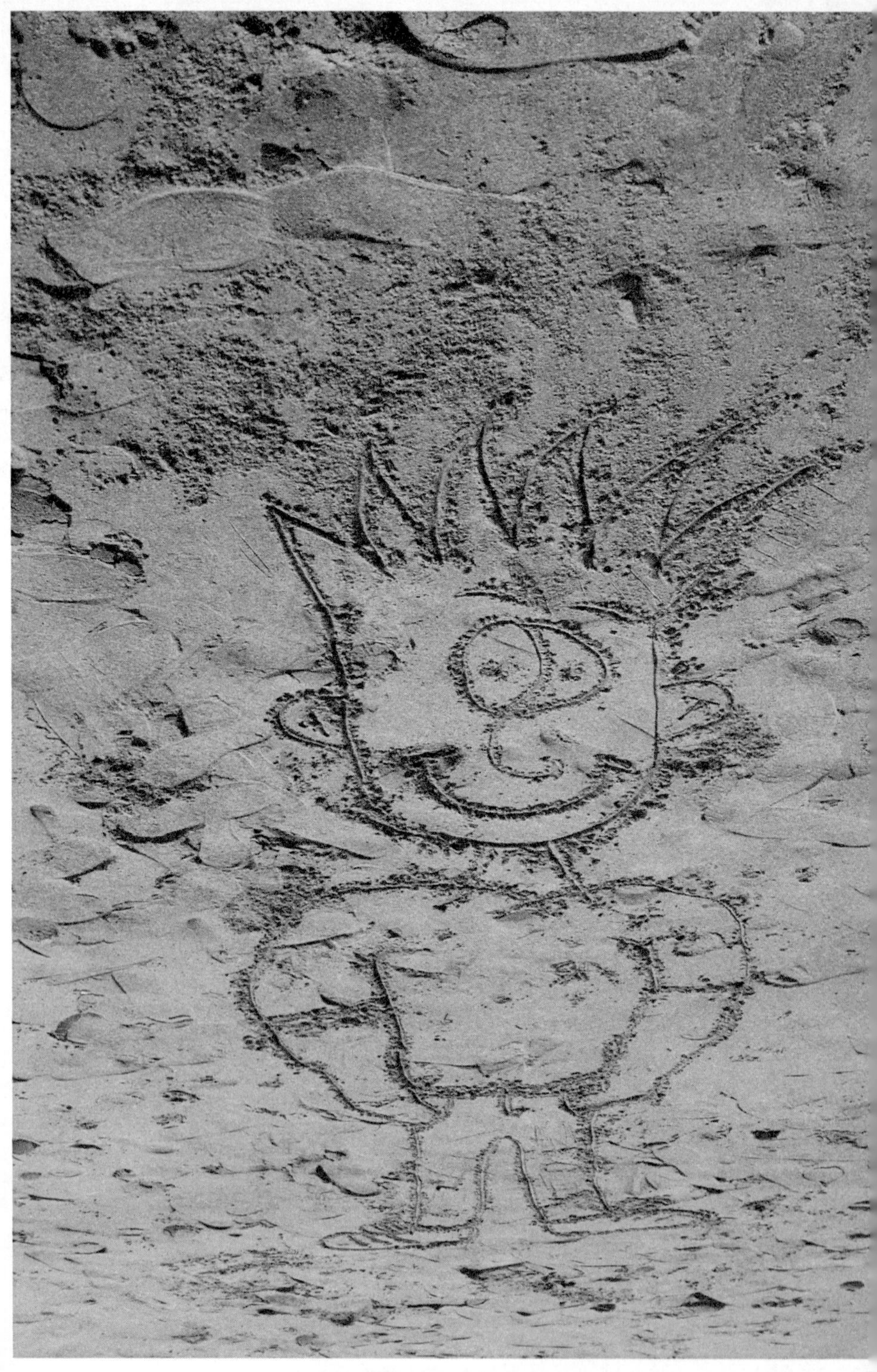

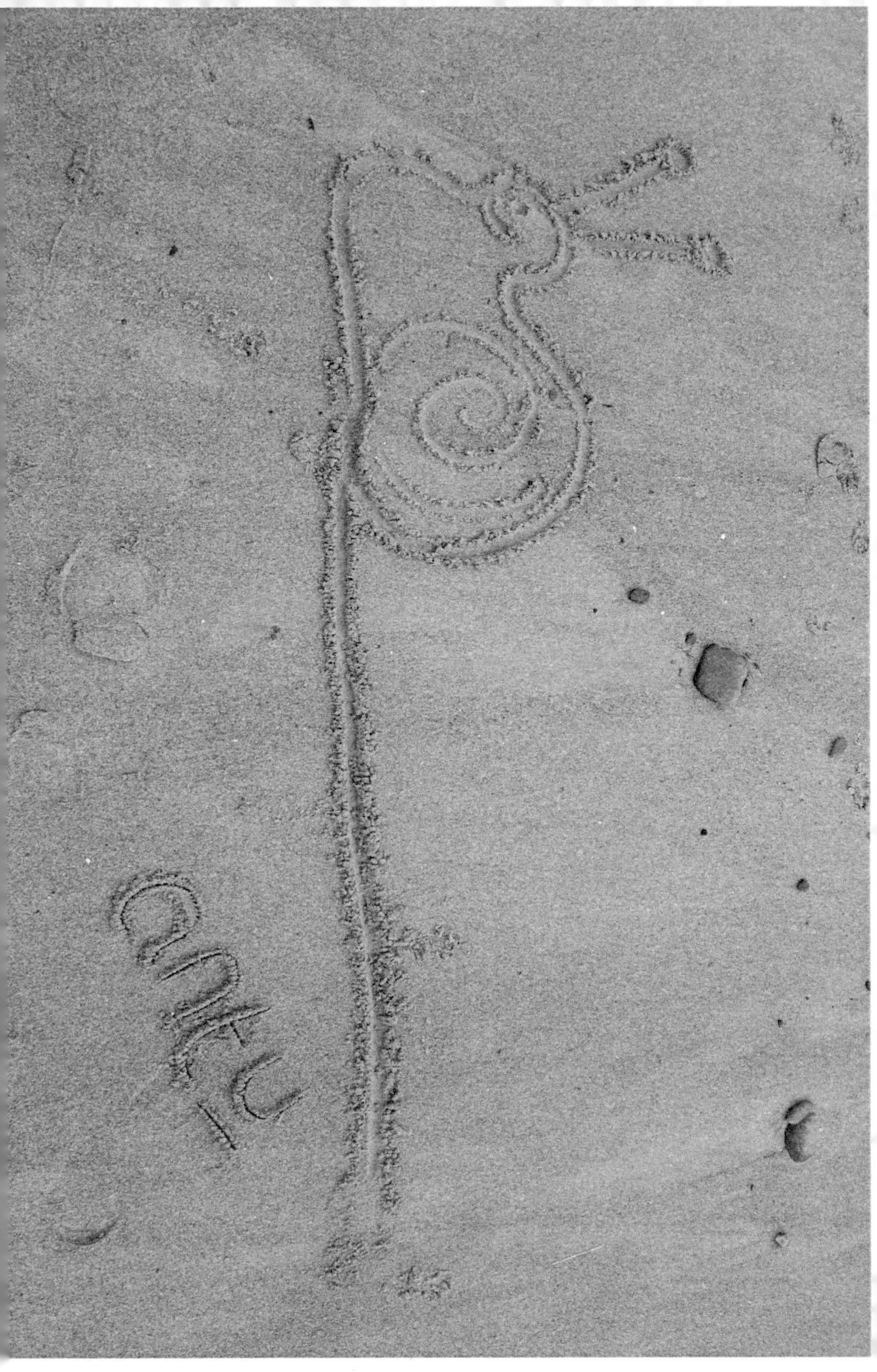

Never Trust A Man Made Of Stones!

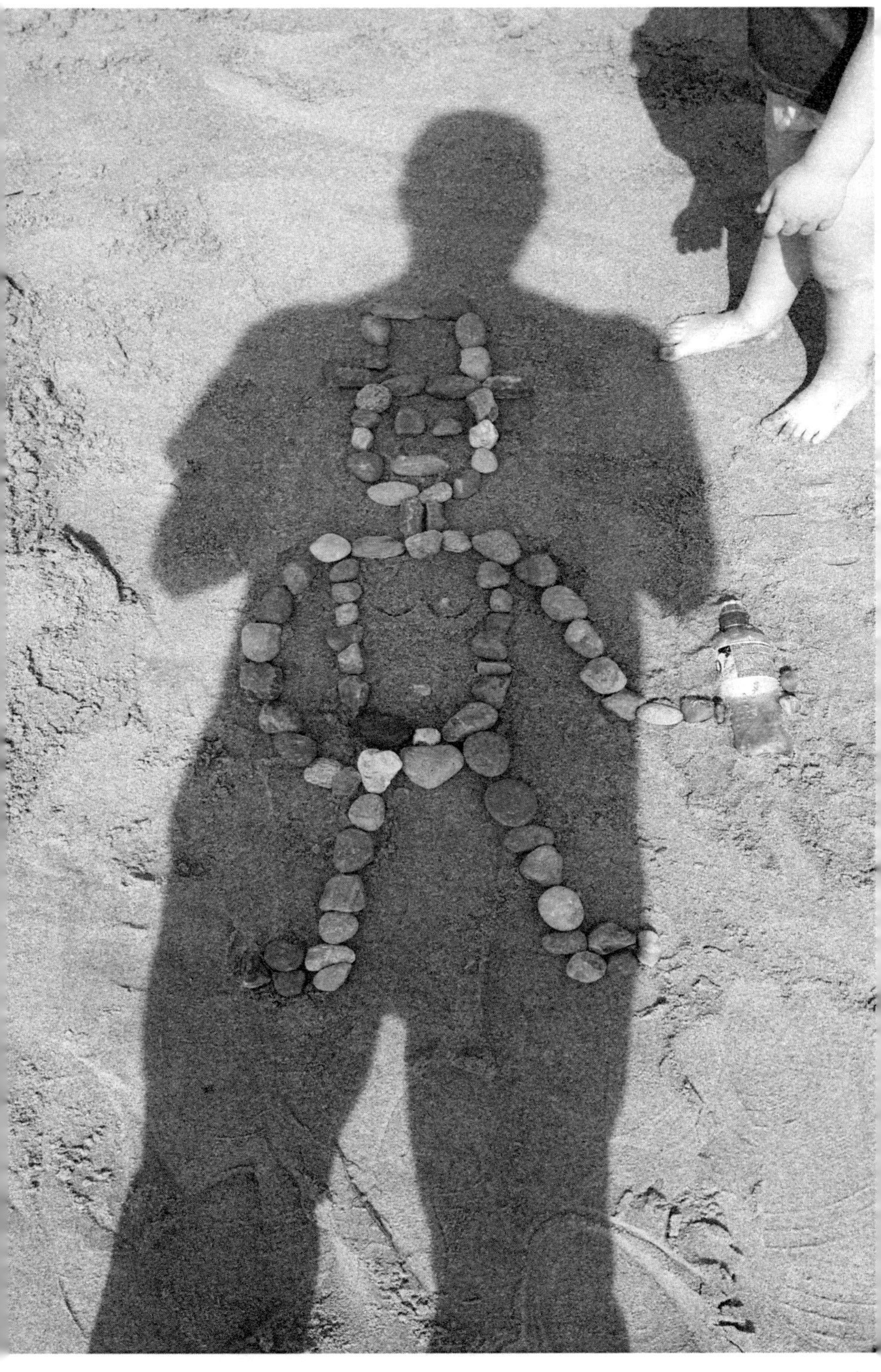

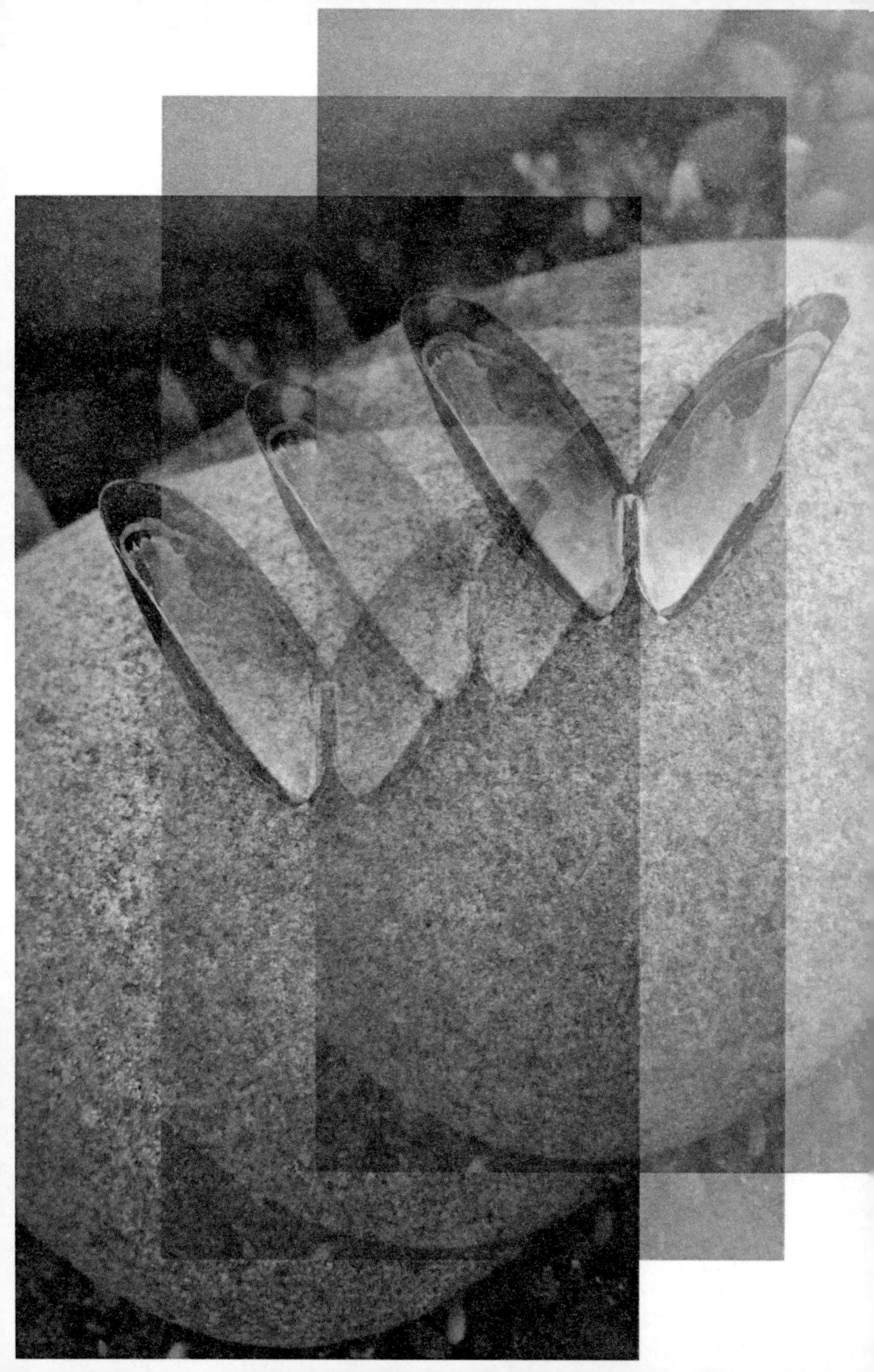

age 25 Incase Anyone Forgot!

anty anty

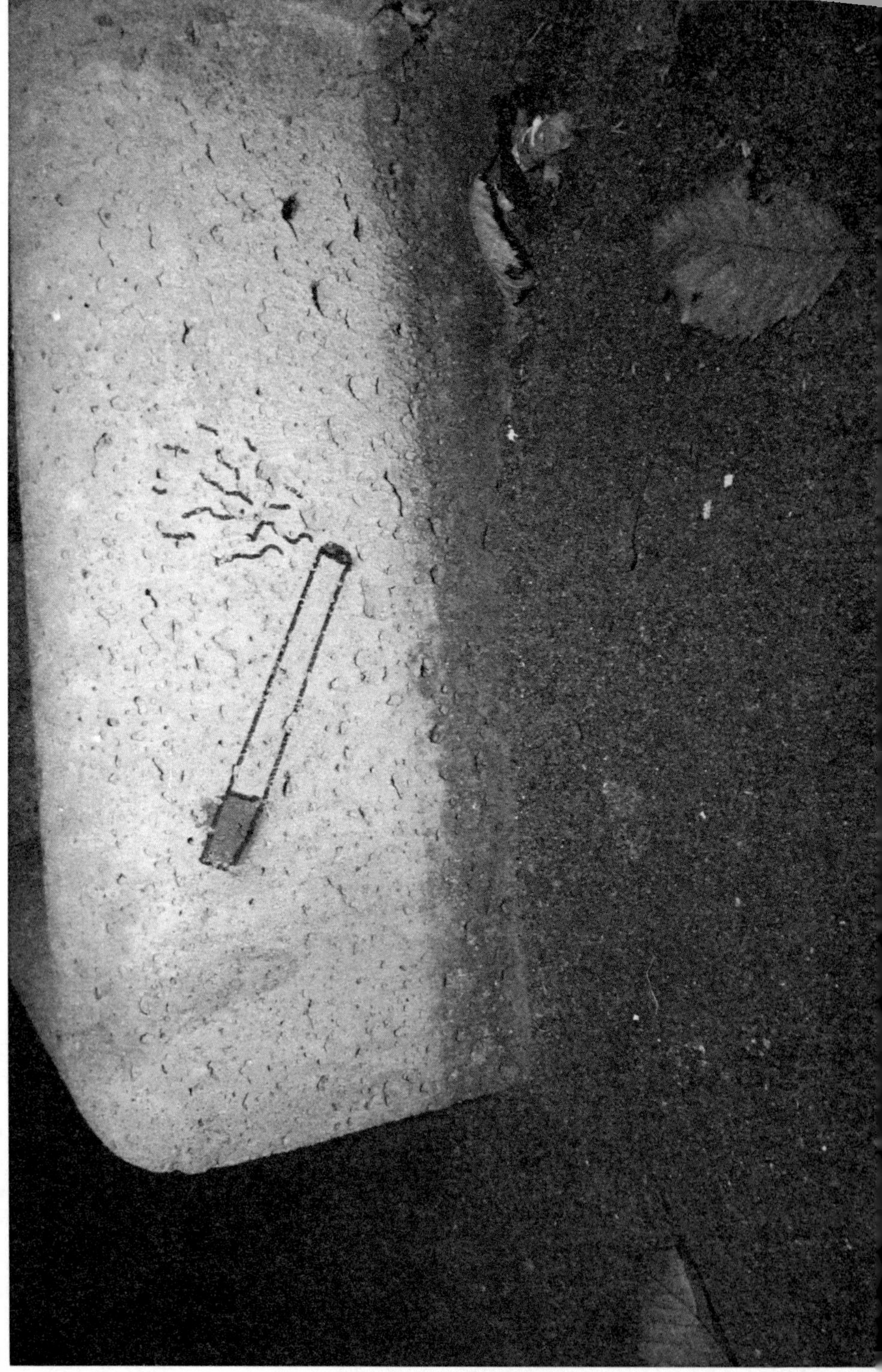

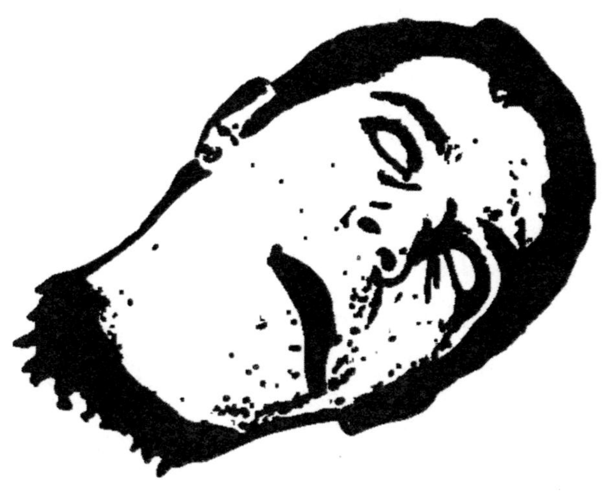

If Found Please
Call Us On
0121 Do ONE!

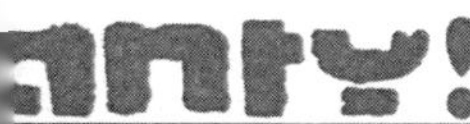

This is Where I Draw the line

anty

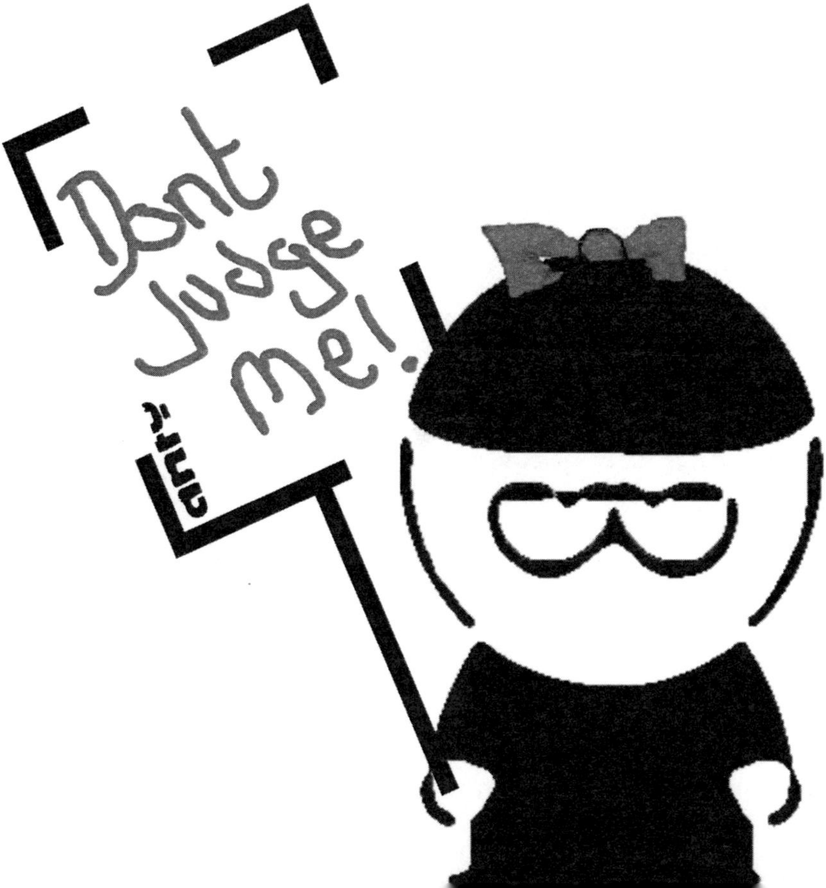

Dont Judge Me!

Free Sweet

Free Sweet

Free Sweet

Never Take A Free Sweet You Never Now Where It's Been!

Putting A Picture Book isn't as Easy as people think!

In my case
it was F*** Easy haha!
really

You May Know This Book Is In No Paticular Order. Its basically showing off all my work in a book format!

I Can't Get Done For Vanderlising My Own Book!

DO YOU HAVE THE RIGHT PIECE!

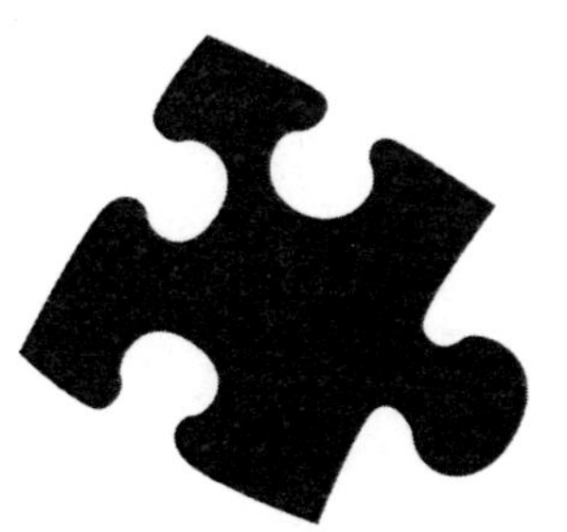

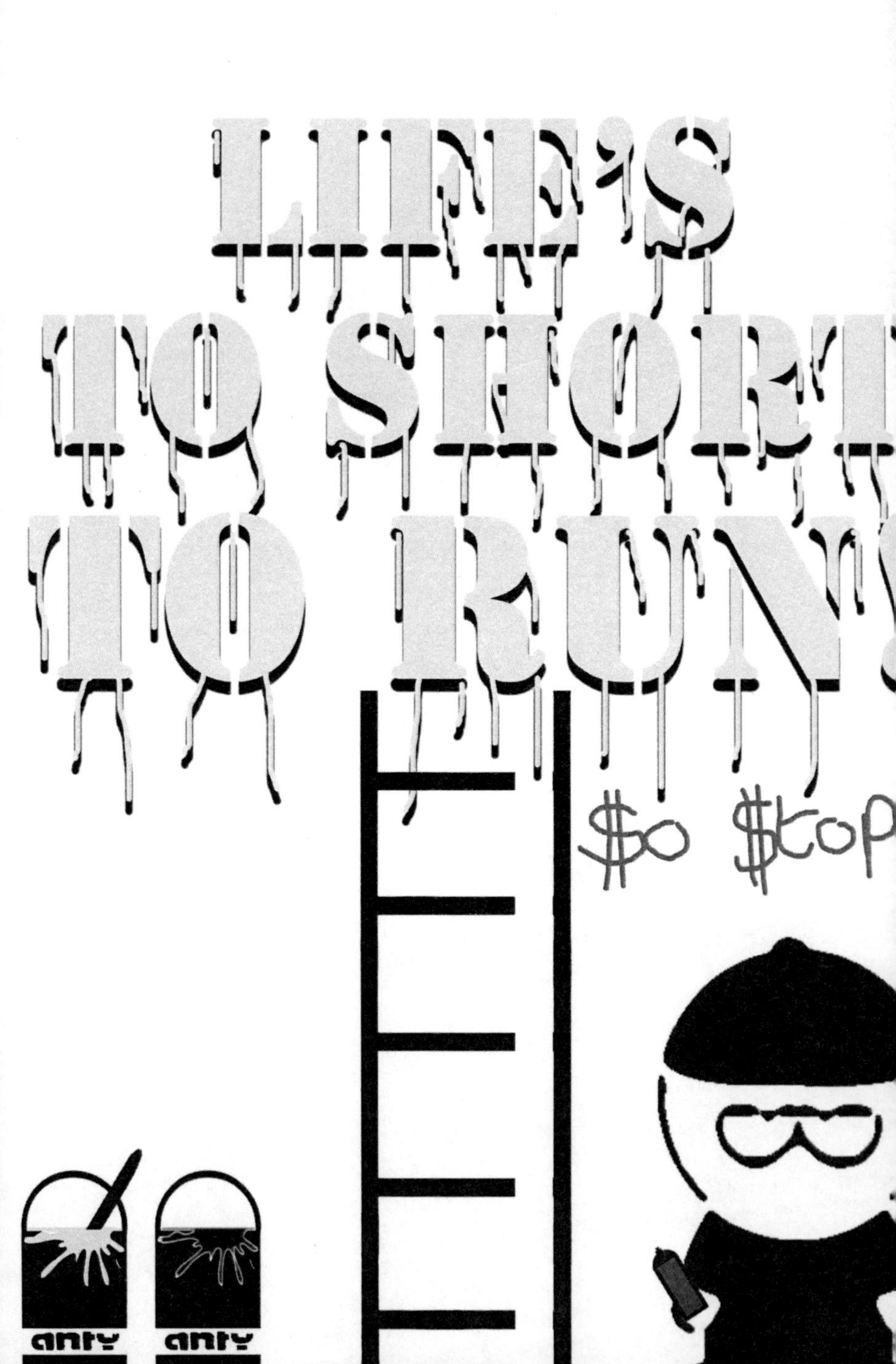
LIFE'S
TO SHORT
TO RUN
$o $top
anty
anty

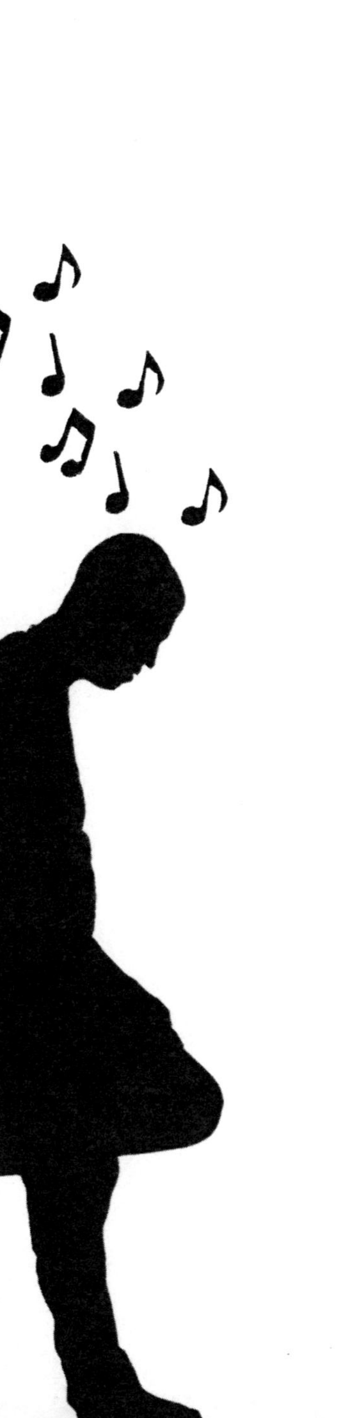

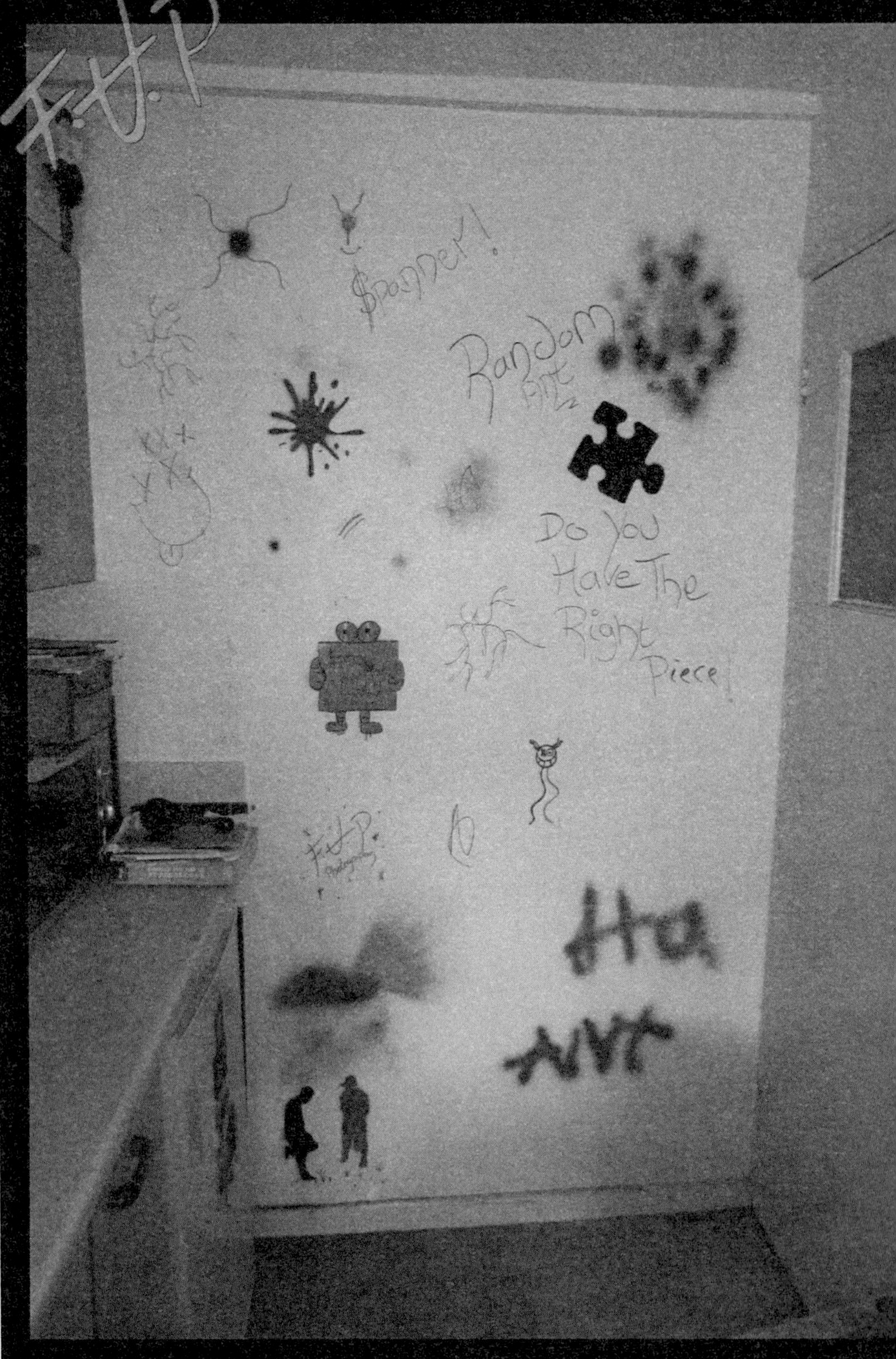
F.U.P
Spanner!
Random Art
Do You Have The Right Piece!
Ha

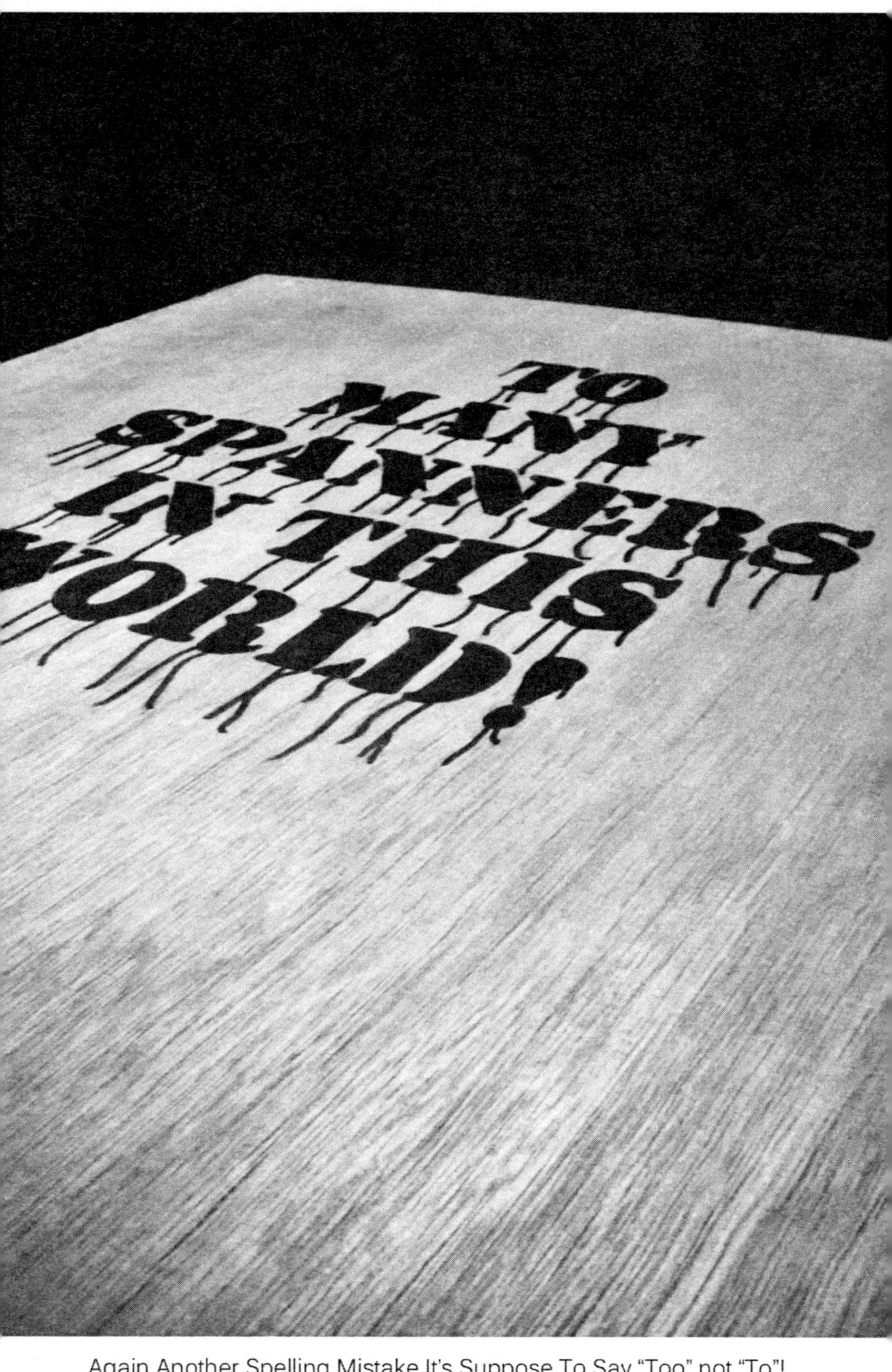

Again Another Spelling Mistake It's Suppose To Say "Too" not "To"!

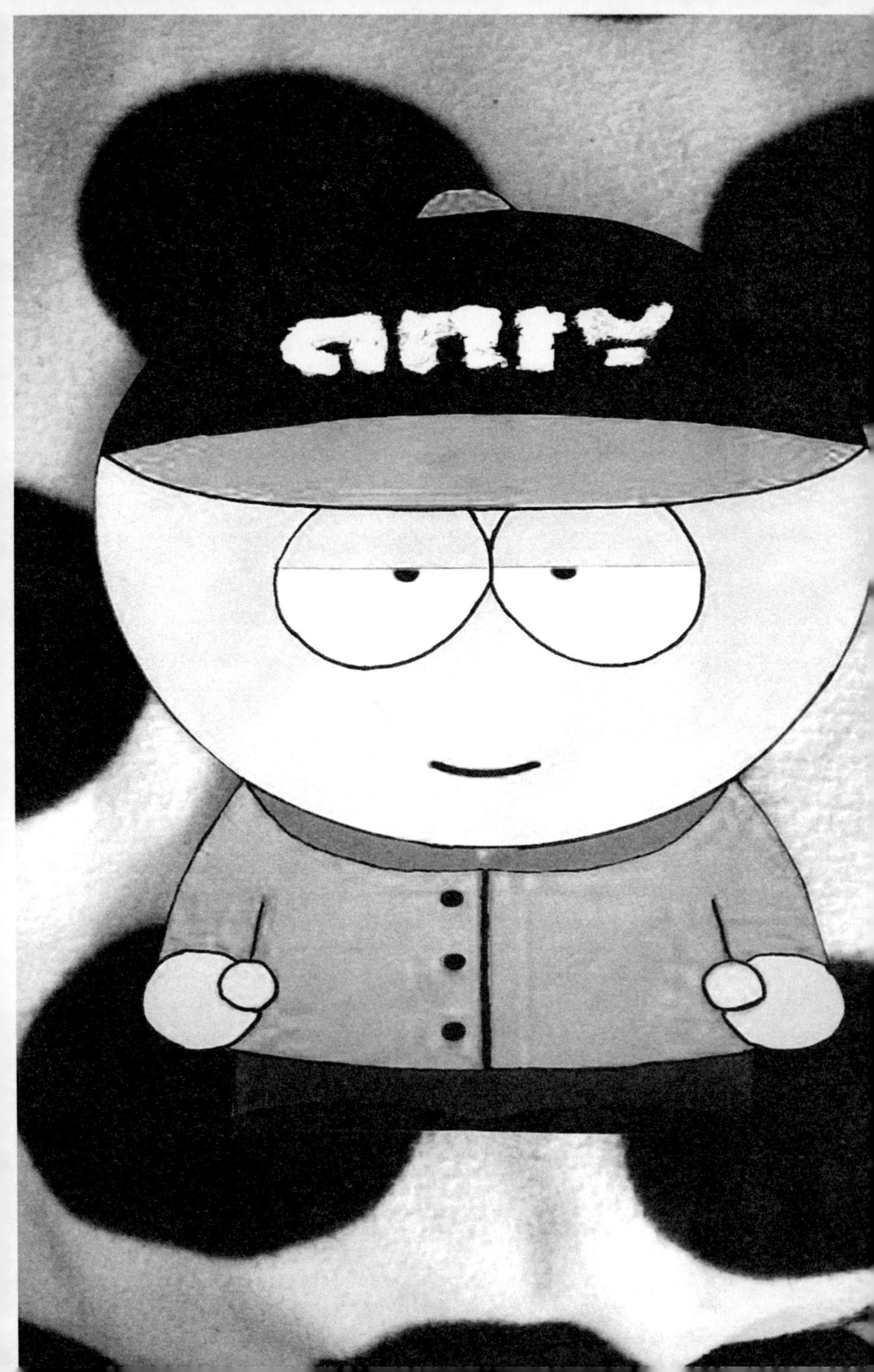

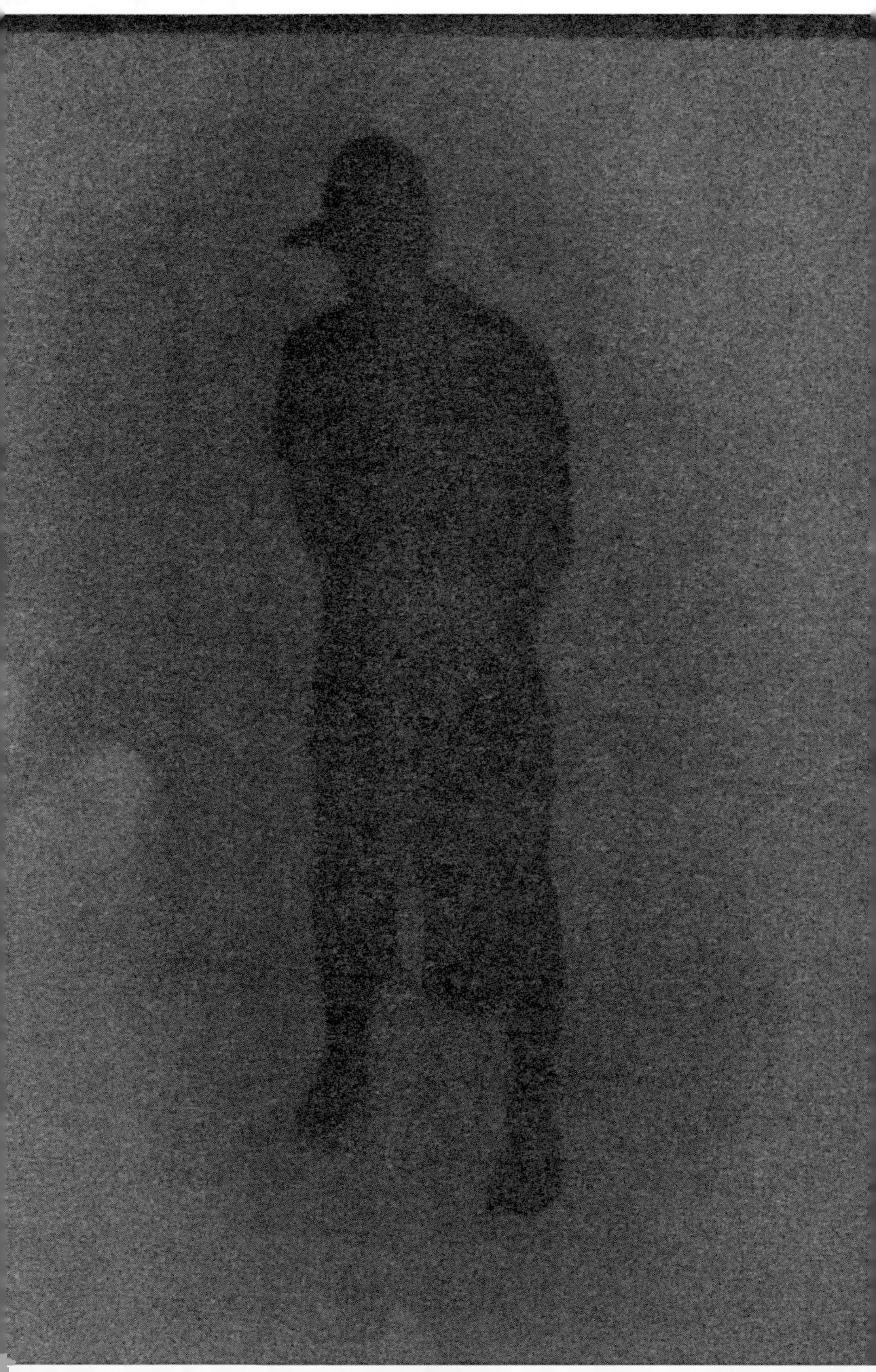

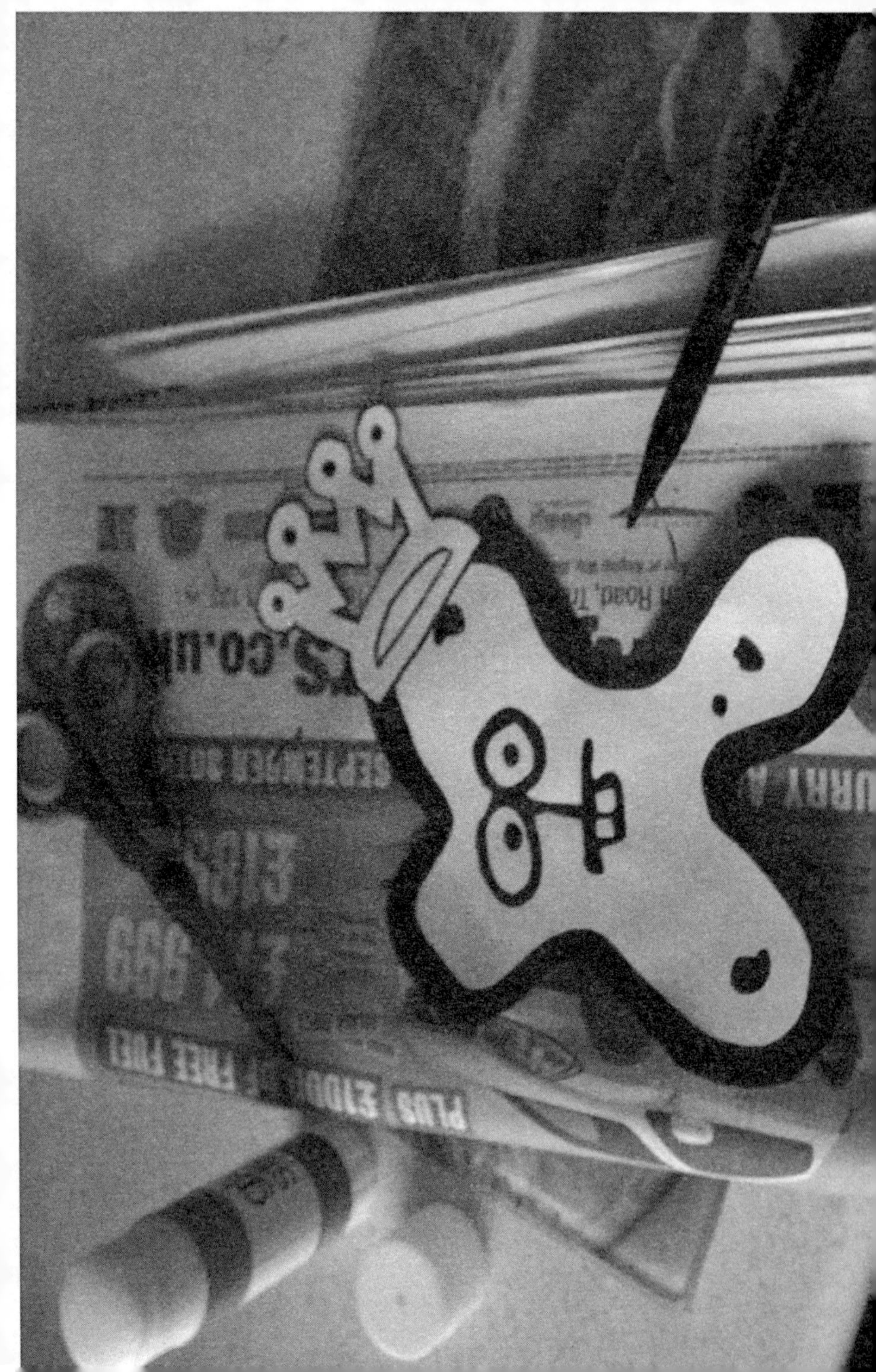

Ever Thought
That The
Planet I$
1 Big Canva$!

That Needs Filling

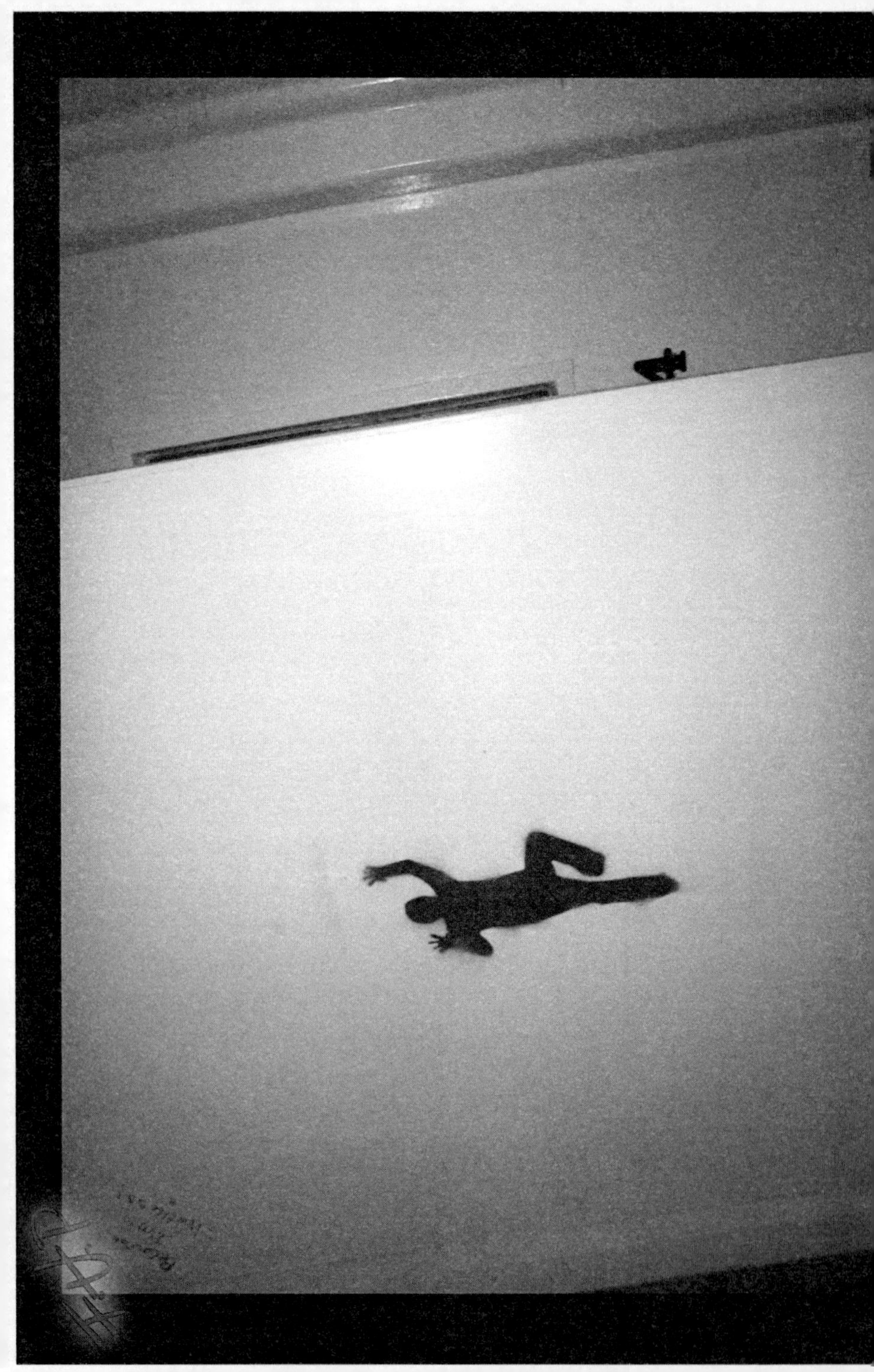

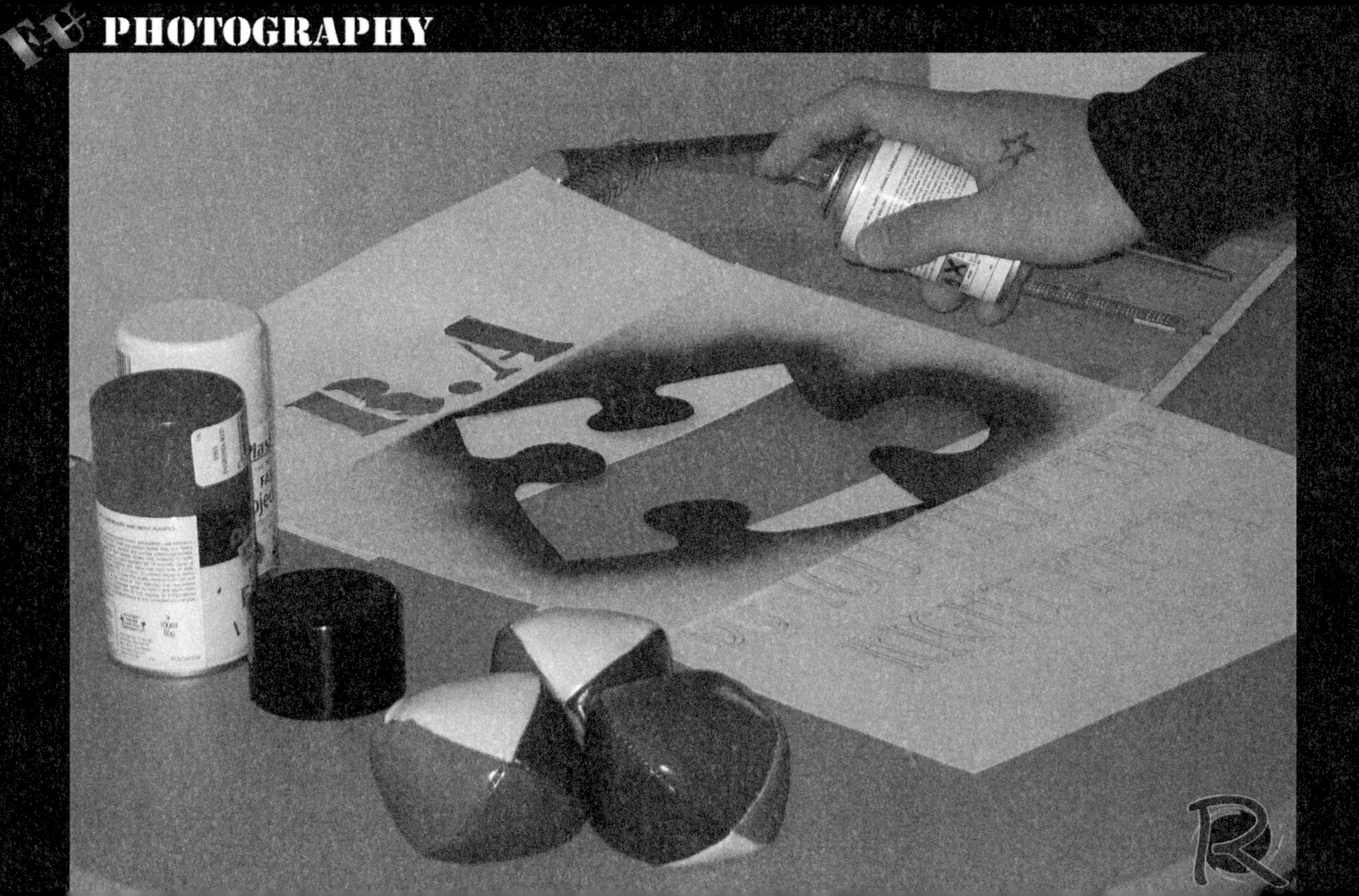
F-U PHOTOGRAPHY

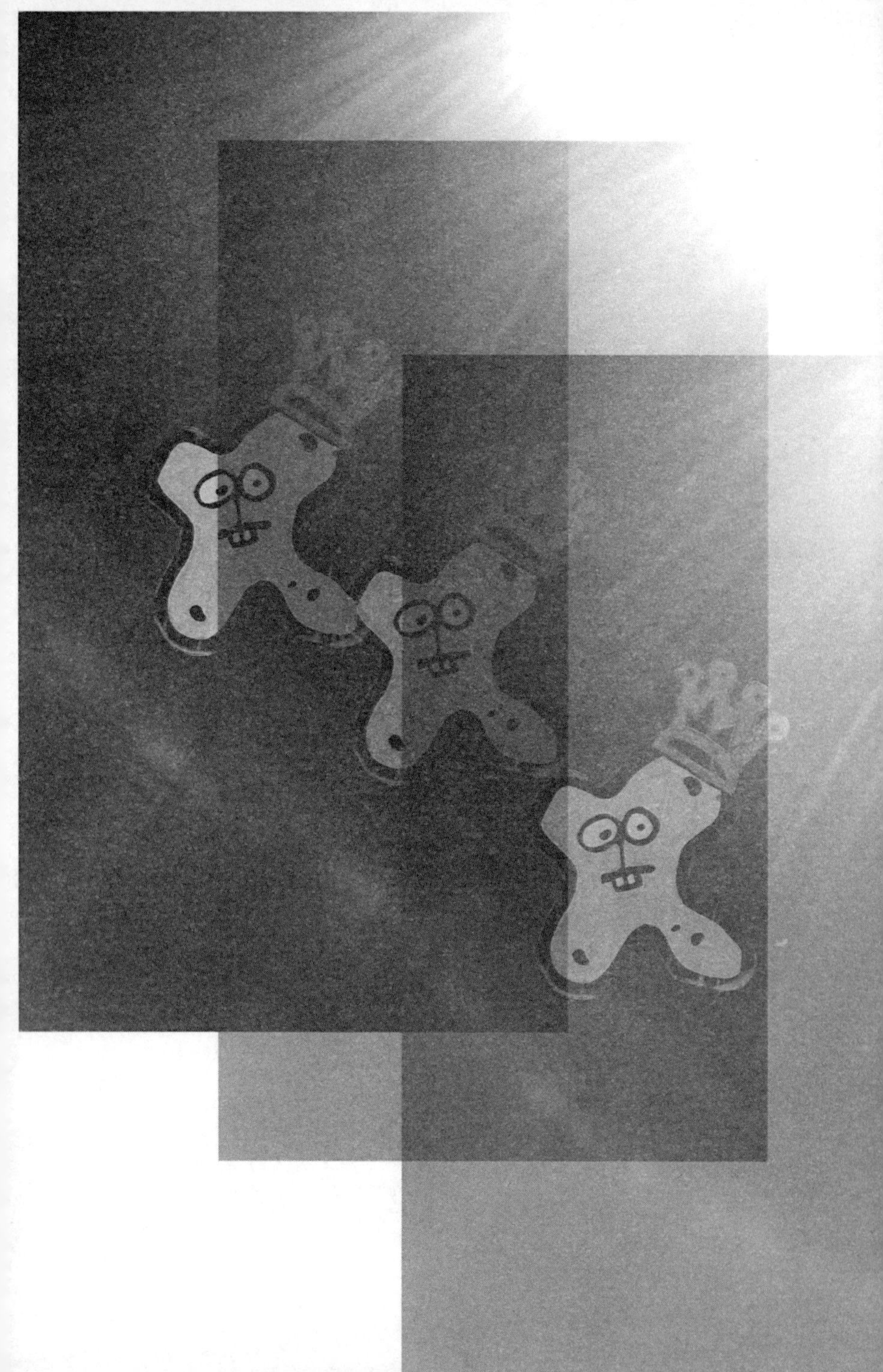

Gloss Black
300ml

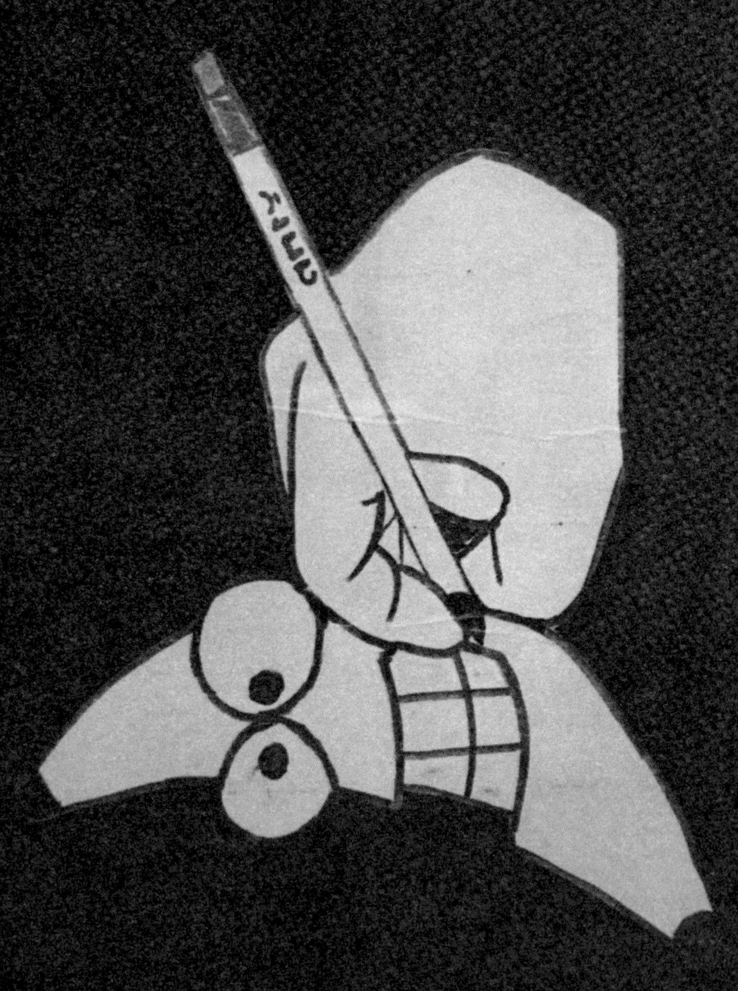

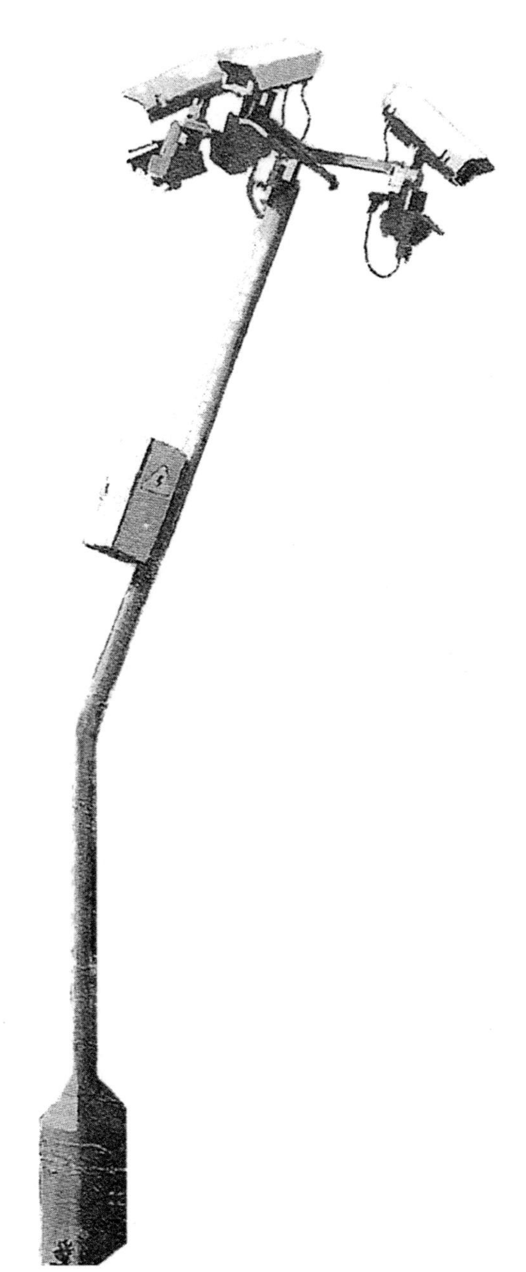

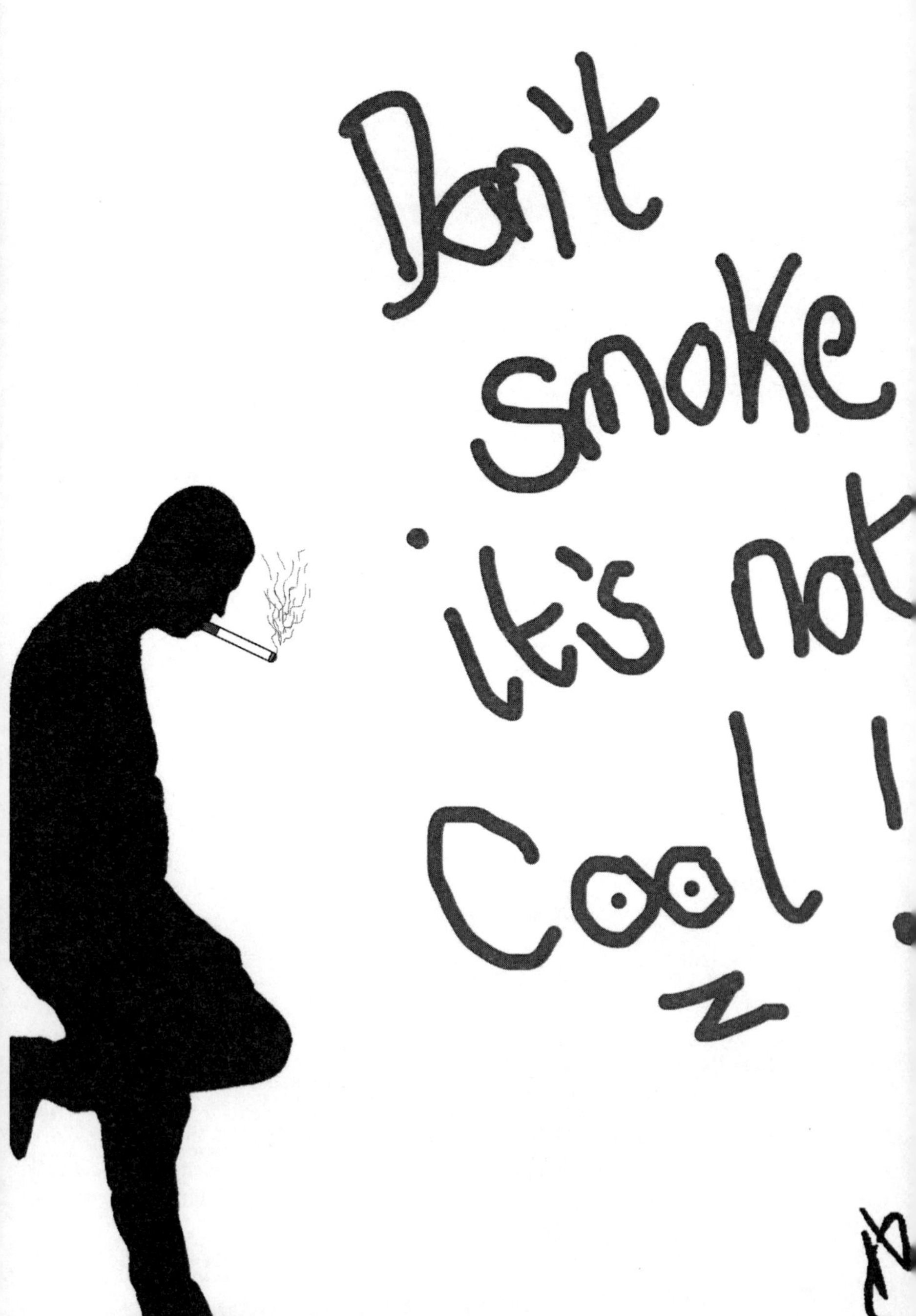
Don't
smoke
it's not
Cool!

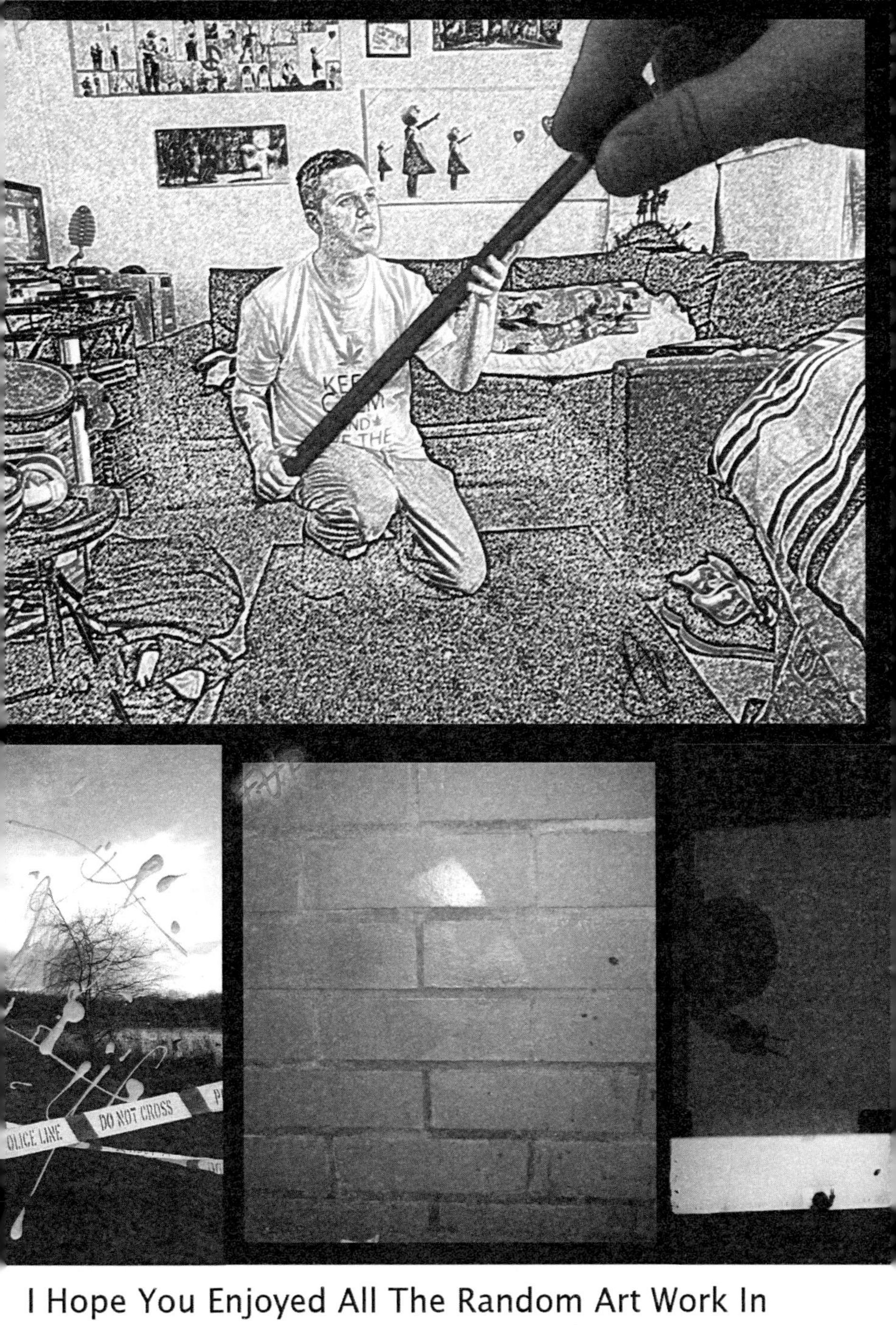

I Hope You Enjoyed All The Random Art Work In This Book.If Anyone Likes Any Of The Designs Or Art Work That's In Here Then Get In Contact? Or Not!

I Really **HOPE** This Book Confused You, **More Than** It Confused **Me** Writing **It** & **Putting** It Together!

Kind Regards Ant Chamberlai

P.S No One Was Harmed In Makin this book happen!

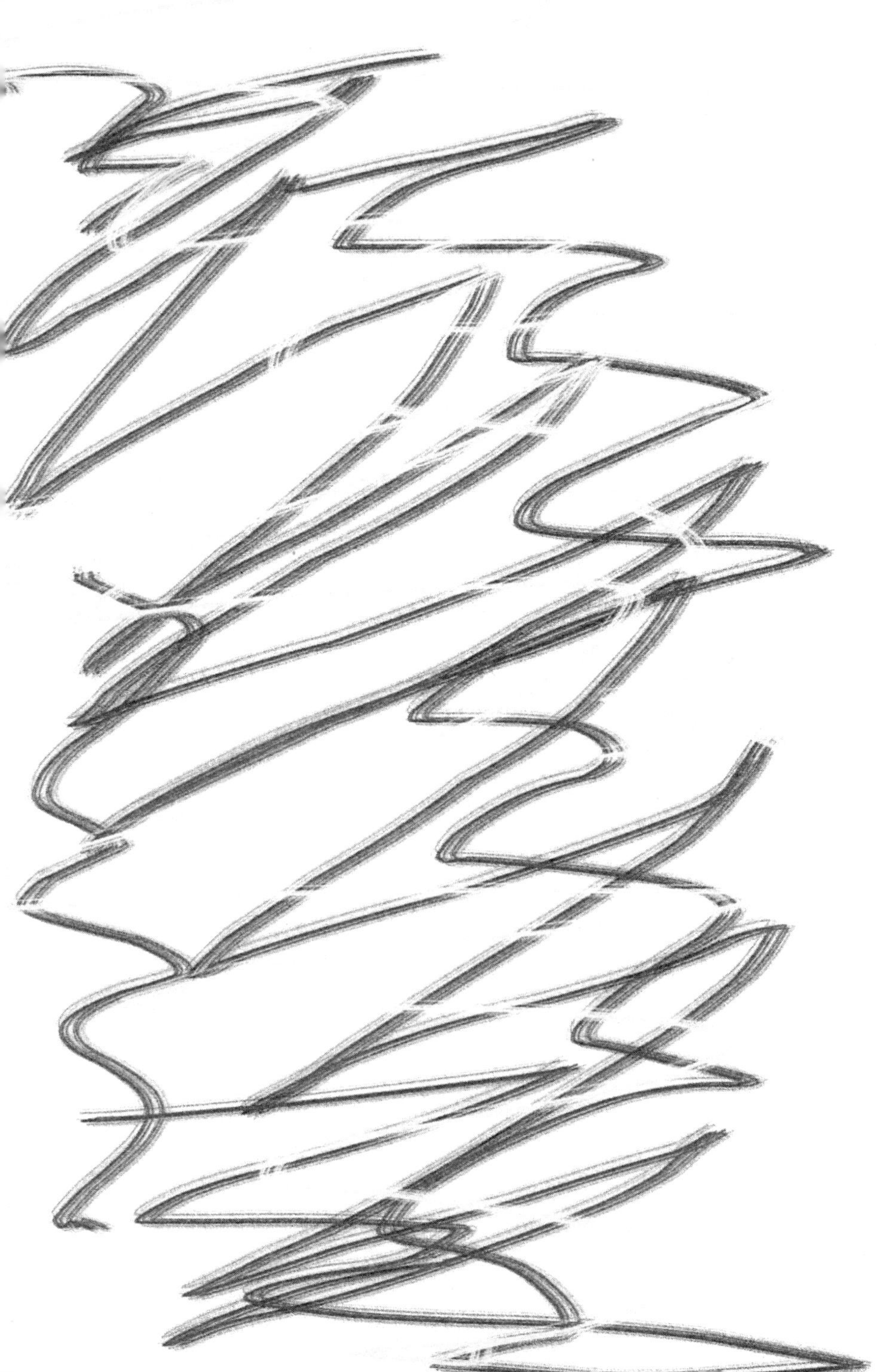

ND - #0275 - 080726 - C0 - 197/132/5 - PB - 9781784562847 - Matt Lamination